SECRETS OF JACOB

DEBRA A. HARKINS

Illustrated by

AUTUMN RAVEN

PURPLE OWL PUBLISHING

Purple Owl Publishing

7 Kingman Rd

Newton, MA 02461

Check out the *Rosen(wald) Descendants* Facebook page. Introduce yourself and stay in touch with our family.

Dedicated to our descendants

May you learn the struggles of the Rozen(wald) family
to avoid repeating the past.

TABLE OF CONTENTS

Acknowledgments 1

Foreword..3

PART I...4

Introduction...5

    James' Ancestors...13

1 - Escapes Anti-Semitism In Poland 14

2 - Crosses Border To UK 39

3 - Marries, Fathers And Works 51

4 - Reaches America And Cuba..73

PART II 81

    Genealogical Family Summaries 82

5 - Parents Sura And Mendel 83

6 - Siblings Adolfo, Itta, Henry And Rosa.......................88

7 - Wives Sarah And Caroline And Children 99

Biography 105

Appendix..106

ACKNOWLEDGMENTS

SYLVIA SARAH ROSEN HARKINS (James daughter) was an incredibly good sport, agreeing to a constant barrage of questions from her daughter Debra. Although Sylvia said she knew little about her father's past, she often remembered small but significant facts and stories her father told her when she was young. Thanks Mom! You made this happen. Caroline Franks Rosen (James 2nd wife) provided invaluable family information to her granddaughter Debra as part of a college genealogy interview assignment just six short months before she died.

MARK (Jimmy) TORBIN (James grandson) who wanted to learn about his namesake, our grandfather James Rosen. Jimmy kept genealogical records on ancestry.com that we were able to use to track down information about James including important details of his first marriage to Jimmy's grandmother, Sarah, and the military records of James and many other relatives in the Rosen family that served in England and the US during WW1, WW2 and the Korean War. I'm not sure this project would be completed without Jimmy's dogged pursuit of those military records.

SARAH ROSEN BIGGINS (James granddaughter) who, along with her son, MATT FOLEY, wanted to learn about the Rosen family line too and shared important documents and photos that she had obtained from her reluctant mother, Dorothy— who understandably did want not to discuss her painful memories. Thank you Sarah, Matt and Dorothy!

RUTH FISCH PADORR (Itta's daughter) is a fellow genealogist and kind soul. She was invaluable in sharing photos of James siblings, conducting phone interviews of Rosa's descendants including daughter Fanny, granddaughter ESTHER HALFRON and grandson JAMES IMIAK. Ruth also willingly shared her recollections of her mother Itta and Ruth's siblings. We owe a huge debt of gratitude to Ruth for generously providing much of the information collected on James siblings and their descendants and introducing us to relatives we never knew existed. Our family grew thru Ruth!

FANNY NOVIGROD (Rosa's daughter) sweetly recalled and shared her memories with Debra (via her son Sal's Spanish-English translation) of her grandparents, Sura and Mendel, her mother Rosa, her Aunt Itta, and her Uncles Adolfo and Henry. Fanny's son SALOMON (Sal) IMIAK (Rosa's grandson) graciously translated between Debra and his mother Fanny while Fanny was in a nursing home in Miami Florida. Sal openly shared the incredible story of how he and his brother, Abraham, were released from Castro's labor camps with the unwavering support of his Aunt Ruth Novigrod. A heartfelt thank you to Fanny and Salomon for sharing even the painful memories with us!

DEBBIE COHEN (Rosa's great granddaughter) who with her father Roberto Cohen—who wanted our family story told too— provided records and photos of Mendel and Sarah and their descendants and willingly shared recollections of James brothers Henry and Adolfo.

GARY BALESTRIERI for his amazing photography help, taking photos of old photos is never easy.

FOREWORD

Before I began working with my cousin Jimmy to research the Rosen side of our family, we each had hit a major roadblock trying to find our maternal grandfather, James Rosen's, birth certificate. Basic questions like: What year was James born? Where was he born? led us to many dead ends, surprises, sadness, anger, happiness and every feeling between.

We learned a lot about our family roots, our connection to the historical suffering of Jewish people, and how and why most of our family ended up in the US, some in the UK and some in Cuba.

Most importantly, we bonded as cousins and found and made connections with family members that we never knew existed and for that we are eternally grateful. Little did we know that the search for our grandfather would reveal so much about the historical exiles of Jews; and of immigrants who so often find themselves caught up in political and religious persecution and violence; and the valiant attempts of those immigrants to find safety for themselves and their families.

Here, we share our journey to find our Rosen roots. Here is our Ashkenazi Jewish immigrant story.

PART I

INTRODUCTION

When the time came for her to give birth, there were twin boys in her womb.

The first to come out was red, and his whole body was like a hairy garment; so, they named him Esau.

After this, his brother came out, with his hand grasping Esau's heel; so, he was named Jacob."

— GENESIS, 25:24-26

The Search for James

Since our maternal grandfather, James Rosen, died in 1960 , before Jimmy was born and when Debra was only 2 years old, we couldn't ask him when and where he was born. Unfortunately, our grandmothers' (yup, we have different grandmothers) had already passed by the time we decided to focus our genealogy research on our Rosen ancestors. Jimmy's mom, Eve (James 2nd daughter) died in 2001. Debra's mom, Sylvia (James youngest daughter), was helpful with some family names and dates that guided our research; but, Sylvia reminded us that her mom and dad did not talk about "such things" like when and where they were born; and she had never thought to ask her father about his family while he was alive.

Jimmy and I started working together to try to find James in early 2017 . Confusion quickly rose when we discovered that James "birth certificate" found within Caroline Rosen (Debra's grandmother, James 2nd wife) personal belongings listed James as Jacob Spivack. Wait, what? Here, check out the birth certificate.

Birth certificate: Jacob Spivack born 4 June 1897 to Mary Scheinfeld and Barnett Spivack in Whitechapel, England

Was Jacob our grandfather's real name and not James? We quickly learned that James is an anglicized version of Jacob; so, we thought *maybe the Spivack birth certificate does belong to our grandfather.* The birthdate seemed to match what Sylvia thought but she was also told that James mother name was Sarah so that did not fit with the birth certificate. Did James wife, Caroline, believe this birth certificate to be James? We think so, since James death certificate which was completed by Caroline identifies James father's name as Barnett--the same name as what appears on the Spivack birth certificate. However, Caroline lists James mother as Sarah. Check out James death certificate below.

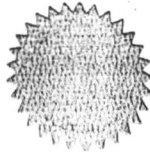

James Rosen death certificate

Initially, we were told by our mothers that James was born in England; but, we could not find him in any of the English birth records. An early family autobiography project[1] Debra completed for one of her doctoral courses in June 1994 indicates that through interviews with her grandmother, Caroline, that James was born in Poland and arrived in England at the age of 9 to live with his uncle. So, the Spivack birth certificate and the family lore was not making sense in many ways including the notion that James was born in England. Jimmy even hired a genealogist to try to find James birth information; but, the genealogist couldn't find our grandfather either. I spoke with a professional genealogist by phone who thought it would be fun for her and her English born genealogist husband to try to find James using the many (costly) databases available to professional genealogists. They searched for James free of charge. However, after three hours, she and her husband were stumped. She said: *"Well this is rare. We don't usually get stumped. You have quite the "red herring"--*which I learned in genealogy parlance means you have a piece of information that doesn't belong, that is not really part of the story. Jimmy and I suspected that it was the Jacob Spivack birth certificate that was the red herring but did not know how to prove it since we could find no other birth certificate for James Rosen. We continued to search for James not knowing the red herring or even whether we had a red herring. So, just imagine our surprise when we found a newspaper clipping tying James Rosen to the name Jacob Spivack.

1964   THE LONDON GAZETTE, 14TH MARCH 1961

aforesaid, FOOTWEAR REPAIRER, and GENERAL DEALER. Court—PLYMOUTH. No. of Matter—5 of 1961. Trustee's Name, Address and Description—Ellis, John Edwin, Ford Park Chambers, Ford Park Road, Plymouth, Chartered Accountant. Date of Certificate of Appointment—10th March, 1961.

HORSEMAN, George, Van Driver, residing at 39, Glamis Walk, West Hartlepool in the county of Durham, and, lately carrying on business at that address and at 36, Brunswick Street, West Hartlepool aforesaid, as a MOBILE GROCER, and formerly residing and carrying on business at 1, Barnard Street, West Hartlepool aforesaid, as an OFF-LICENSEE and GENERAL DEALER. Court—STOCKTON-ON-TEES. No. of Matter—2 of 1961. Trustee's Name, Address and Description—Cook, John Alan, Barrington House, 2, Bowesfield Lane, Stockton-on-Tees, Chartered Accountant. Date of Certificate of Appointment—9th March, 1961.

RELEASE OF TRUSTEES

COOK, Sylvia (married woman), trading as " Dyne Engineering Co.," residing at Ambassadors Hotel, Meyrick Road, Bournemouth, Hants, and lately carrying on business at 17-23, Lonsdale Road, Kilburn, N.W.6, London, MACHINE TOOL MANUFACTURER. Court—HIGH COURT OF JUSTICE. No. of Matter—464 of 1950. Trustee's Name, Address and Description—Macleod, Torquil John Murdoch, Chartered Accountant, 4, Bucklersbury, London, E.C.4. Date of Release—3rd March, 1961.

DOBBS, Raymond, of 2, Station Road, Waunlwyd, Ebbw Vale in the county of Monmouth, Steelworks Labourer, lately carrying on business as a BUILDER, at 2, Station Road, Waunlwyd, Ebbw Vale aforesaid. Court—BLACKWOOD, TREDEGAR and ABERTILLERY. No. of Matter—10 of 1959. Trustee's Name, Address and Description—Meredith, Walter Harold, County Court Buildings (First Floor), Westgate Street, Cardiff, Official Receiver. Date of Release—9th March, 1961.

THOMPSON, Gladys, (married woman), of 17, Oakland Road, Rodley in the city of Leeds, lately carrying on business at 3, Rodley Lane, Rodley aforesaid, under the name or style of " Pat Thompson ", LADIES and CHILDREN'S OUTFITTER. Court—BRADFORD. No. of Matter—6 of 1959. Trustee's Name, Address and Description—Williams, John Lewis, 20, North Parade, Bradford, Official Receiver. Date of Release—8th March, 1961.

BEECH, Reginald Gilbert, residing and carrying on business at 21, Bedford Place, Brighton in the county of Sussex, under the style of " Salon de Gilbert " as a LADIES HAIRDRESSER. Court—BRIGHTON. No. of Matter—15 of 1960. Trustee's Name, Address and Description—Parker, Thomas Henry, 8, Old Steine, Brighton, 1, Official Receiver. Date of Release—10th March, 1961.

DARE, Frederick Victor, of 36a, Pawsons Road, West Croydon in the county of Surrey, BUILDER, and PAYNE, Frederick John, of 42J, Lodge Hill, New Addington, Croydon in the county of Surrey, BUILDER, lately trading together as D. & P. Builders, (a firm), at 42J, Lodge Hill, New Addington, Croydon in the county of Surrey, BUILDERS, lately carrying on business at 3, Bracken Avenue, Shirley, Croydon in the county of Surrey. Court—CROYDON. No. of Matter—35 of 1959. Trustee's Name, Address and Description—Hill, William Joseph Wallis, 58-61, York Terrace, Regent's Park, London, N.W.1 (Official Receiver). Date of Release—9th March, 1961.

BONSALL, Stanley, of 7, Church Walk, Eastwood in the county of Nottingham, BUILDER and CONTRACTOR, lately residing at and carrying on business at 44, Park Crescent, Eastwood aforesaid, and previously residing and carrying on business at 44, Park Crescent, Eastwood aforesaid and previously residing and carrying on business at 113, (renumbered 111), Main Road, Underwood in the

said county of Nottingham. Court—DERBY and LONG EATON. No. of Matter—13 of 1959. Trustee's Name, Address and Description—Jordan, Walter William, 27, Regent Street, Park Row, Nottingham, Official Receiver. Date of Release—10th March, 1961.

PHILO, Sydney Joseph, of 171, Normanshire Drive, Chingford in the county of Essex, TRAVELLER. Court—EDMONTON. No. of Matter—17 of 1958. Trustee's Name, Address and Description—Whitehead, Wilfred, 58-61, York Terrace, Regent's Park, London, N.W.1, Official Receiver. Date of Release—8th March, 1961.

CONDON, Michael John, of 40, North Parade, Halifax in the county of York, no occupation, but lately carrying on business as a CAFE PROPRIETOR, at 40, North Parade, Halifax aforesaid. Court—HALIFAX. No. of Matter—3 of 1959. Trustee's Name, Address and Description—Williams, John Lewis, 20, North Parade, Bradford, 1, Official Receiver. Date of Release—8th March, 1961.

ANDERTON, Monica Audrey, (married woman), residing at 71, Green Lane, Ilkeston in the county of Derby, lately residing and carrying on business at 93-95, Sneinton Boulevard in the city of Nottingham, as a GROCER, and GENERAL STORE PROPRIETOR. Court—NOTTINGHAM. No. of Matter—43 of 1959. Trustee's Name, Address and Description—Jordan, Walter William, 27, Regent Street, Park Row, Nottingham, Official Receiver. Date of Release—10th March, 1961.

EWEN, George, of Priory Cottage, High Road, Fobbing, Stanford-le-Hope in the county of Essex, carrying on business as a BUTCHER and GROCER, under the style of Halston Stores, (J. Ewen), at High Road, Fobbing, Stanford-le-Hope aforesaid, (described in the Receiving Order as a Butcher, Grocer and Draper). Court—SOUTHEND. No. of Matter—34 of 1959. Trustee's Name, Address and Description—Clifford, John Basil, Chartered Accountant, 4, Bucklersbury, London, E.C.4. Date of Release—24th Feb., 1961.

THOMSETT, George Herbert, Clare, 14, Plough Lane Close, Wallington, Surrey, lately residing and carrying on business at 123, Camden Road, Tunbridge Wells, Kent, as a CAFE PROPRIETOR. Court—TUNBRIDGE WELLS. No. of Matter—9 of 1959. Trustee's Name, Address and Description—Parker, Thomas Henry, 8, Old Steine, Brighton 1, Official Receiver. Date of Release—10th March, 1961.

INTENDED DIVIDENDS

LOODMER, John Bernard, formerly of 78, Wigmore Street, London, W.1, but whose present address is unknown. MANUFACTURER of LADIES WEAR. Court—HIGH COURT OF JUSTICE. No. of Matter—879 of 1954. Last Day for Receiving Proofs—28th March, 1961. Name of Trustee and Address—Vaz, J. J. Nunes, C.A., Balfour House, Finsbury Pavement, London, E.C.2.

SPEVACK, Jacob (commonly known as James Rosen), described in the Receiving Order as James Rosen, of 220, Arlington Road, London, N.W.1, lately of 32, Fountayne Road, London, N.16, and lately carrying on business as 1, Rosen, at 64, Christian Street, London, E.1, LADIES TAILOR. Court—HIGH COURT OF JUSTICE. No. of Matter—386 of 1948. Last Day for Receiving Proofs—28th March, 1961. Name of Trustee and Address—Walter, Arthur Aaron, Bankruptcy Buildings, Carey Street, London, W.C.2, Official Receiver.

EVANS, Noel Griffith, residing at 6, Gambier Terrace, Garth Road, Bangor in the county of Caernarvon, of no occupation. Court—BANGOR. No. of Matter—12 of 1955. Last Day for Receiving Proofs—28th March, 1961. Name of Trustee and Address—Pagan, Ronald William Francis, West Africa House, 25, Water Street, Liverpool 2, Official Receiver.

James Rosen aka Jacob Spivack

Our confusion continued when we obtained James marriage certificate to his 1st wife Sarah Reuben (Jimmy's grandmother) from 1918 and the marriage certificate to his 2nd wife, Caroline Franks (Debra's grandmother) from 1939. We noticed that James identified his father as Solomon Rosen in 1918 but as Mendel Rosen in 1939. Also, he used the name Jacob, aka James, in the 1939 marriage document. We decided that

James was a *scallywag!* Yup, we were frustrated. If you're still following along with all these names, you'll notice that at this point, we had three names for James father: Barnett, Solomon, and Mendel; two names for his mother: Mary and Sarah; and two names for James himself: James Rosen and Jacob Spivack. Changing his name and his parents' names willy-nilly from one document to another, our grandfather was driving us crazy from the grave.

James Rosen marriage to Sarah Reuben 1 Sept 1918

James (aka Jacob) Rosen marriage to Caroline Franks 24 December 1939

We were running out of ideas of ever figuring out who was our grandfather when a woman named Ruth Padorr from Miami, Florida contacted us via email and said she believed we were related. Ruth said her mom grew up in

Cuba but that her mother—Itta Rosenwald and family—were originally from Poland. Ruth said the family <u>always</u> went by the surname Rosenwald and that the parents of James and her mother Itta were Sura and Mendel Rosenwald.

Hmph...We're not Rosenwalds, we're Rosens! Ruth is confused. Yes, we were in denial.

Except, it turns out that Ruth and I had copies of the same old photo. My photo originally belonged to my grandmother, Caroline, and on the back of the photo it said *James parents;* while Ruth's photo had originally belonged to her mother, Itta, and her colorized photo version of the same photo always hung in Ittas' living room. Who were the people in that photo? Meet James and Ittas' parents, our great grandparents, Sura and Mendel Rosenwald.

Sura and Mendel Rosenwald

Shaul Stampfer[2] wrote that in 19th Century Jewish Eastern Europe *"The ideal man was the retiring, pale, delicate, Talmudist, with sensitive hands and long white fingers, while the ideal woman was an active, even aggressive, full-bodied woman with multiple chins."* As can be seen in the photo above and in recollections by their granddaughter, Fanny, Grandpa Mendel was a smallish more delicate man while Grandma Sura was a full-bodied woman. James parents, our great grandparents, were the ideal 19th Century Eastern European Jewish couple!

Although we wanted to believe that Sura and Mendel were our great grandparents, Jimmy and I were still a bit skeptical as we still had no legal documents to prove the family connection to Ruth—who told us that these were James parents—we still had several documents with two different names for James and differing names for his parents. Our skepticism finally ended when our genetic results from *23andMe* confirmed that Ruth Fische Padoor (daughter of Itta Rosenwald) is a first cousin of Sylvia Sarah Rosen Harkins (daughter of James Rosen).

We were both excited and confused by this genetic realization. Excited to finally find someone that we were related to on the Rosen side of our family and confused for many reasons. We were excited to know that James parents had lived in Cuba and that he had siblings who lived in Cuba. Sylvia was stunned; and we were excited to learn that we had at least one great aunt and several cousins in Cuba. Simultaneously, we had an explosion of questions that we now needed to explore. Why did James never speak about his parents and siblings in Cuba? Did James know where his parents and siblings were? Did James parents know that he was living in England? Why did James have an alias? Why was James using the surname Rosen while the rest of his family used the surname Rosenwald? Why was James in England and his family in Cuba? Why did his mother and father leave him in England when he was so young? Why did James parents take his siblings to Cuba and not James? How did James get to England from Poland? When did James and his parents leave Poland? Why did James family leave Poland?

We tell you our genealogy attempts to find James because it turns out that our grandfather's story is the story of many Jews during this historical period, it is a story shrouded in Jewish persecution and exile. We begin our story with James parents in Poland.

---

1. 1994 autobiography paper in Debra's papers.
2. Source: Stampfer, Shaul 1992. Gender differentiation and education of Jewish woman in 19th Century Eastern Europe. Polin: Studies in Polish Jewry, 7: 63-87

JAMES' ANCESTORS

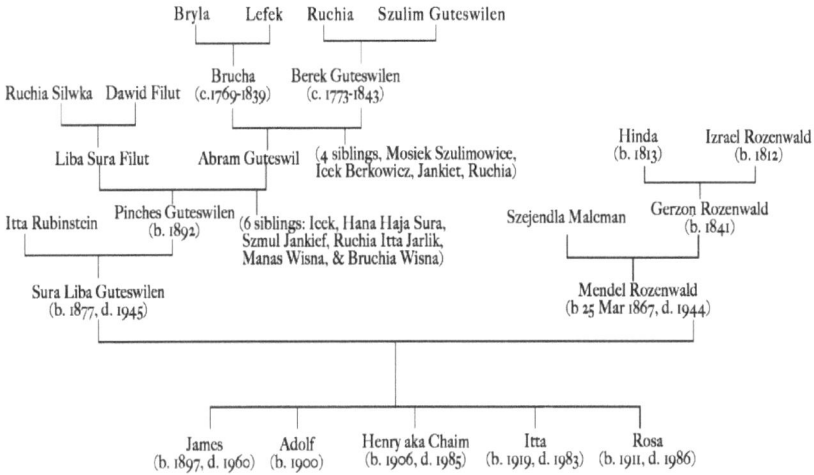

Bryla — Lefek   Ruchia — Szulim Guteswilen

Brucha (c.1769-1839) — Berek Guteswilen (c. 1773-1843)

Ruchia Silwka — Dawid Filut

Hinda (b. 1813) — Izrael Rozenwald (b. 1812)

Liba Sura Filut — Abram Guteswil   (4 siblings, Mosiek Szulimowice, Icek Berkowicz, Jankiet, Ruchia)

Itta Rubinstein — Pinches Guteswilen (b. 1892)   (6 siblings: Icek, Hana Haja Sura, Szmul Jankief, Ruchia Itta Jarlik, Manas Wisna, & Bruchia Wisna)

Szejendla Malcman — Gerzon Rozenwald (b. 1841)

Sura Liba Guteswilen (b. 1877, d. 1945) — Mendel Rozenwald (b 25 Mar 1867, d. 1944)

James (b. 1897, d. 1960)   Adolf (b. 1900)   Henry aka Chaim (b. 1906, d. 1985)   Itta (b. 1919, d. 1983)   Rosa (b. 1911, d. 1986)

1

ESCAPES ANTI-SEMITISM IN POLAND

"If you prick us, do we not bleed? If you tickle us, do we not laugh? If you poison us, do we not die?"

— WILLIAM SHAKESPEARE, THE MERCHANT OF VENICE
(ACT III, SCENE I)

Antisemitism in Poland

Antisemitism can be traced to the time of Christ and sadly continues to the present day. Each time antisemitism arose during the past 2,000 years, Jews were forced to leave their home and find a new place to live. For hundreds of years, Poland was the most tolerant Eastern European country until it wasn't.

Poland's1 unique tolerance for Jews

Poland represents the birthplace of *Ashkenazi*, or the Jewish Eastern European culture. Locked between the then superpowers Prussia, Austria and Russia, Poland was the most culturally diverse country in Europe during the 16th and 17th century, a tolerant cultural oasis surrounded by a vast expanse of religious intolerance on all sides. Not only did Poland have the largest Jewish populations of any country before WW1, there were large numbers of non-Christian, Protestant and Unitarian religious sects that settled there seeking similar religious respite from Christian zealots (Polonsky, 2013[2]). Note, the movement into Poland beginning in the 10th Century all the way through the 14th Century as Jewish expulsion continued throughout Europe as Christianity expanded (See Figure 1).

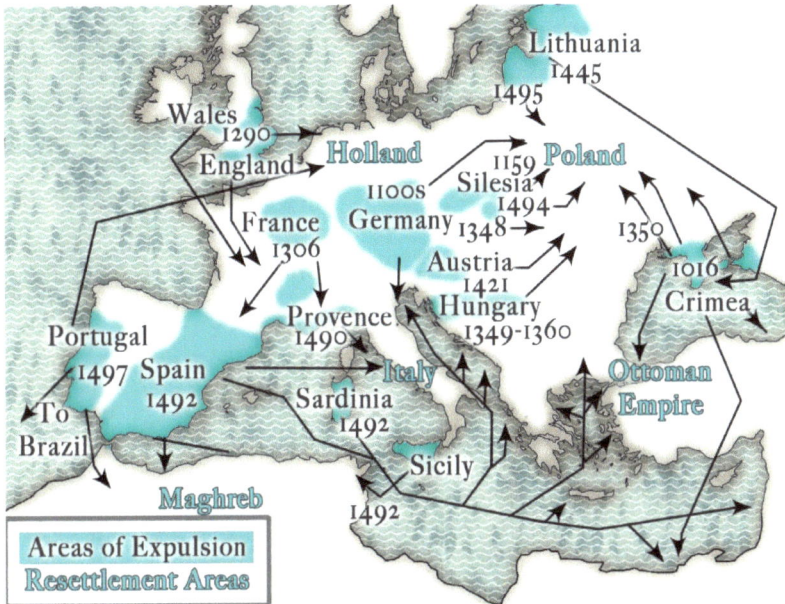

Figure 1: https://fcit.usf.edu/holocaust/people/displace.htm

Jews are an ethnoreligious group that can trace their ancestry back to the ancient Israelites of Levant. Religious and political persecution is a sadly defining feature of the Jewish people dating back to before the 8th C BCE. The Jews experienced at least two Diasporas or dispersion of the Jews out of their ancestral motherland and their eventual settlement across the globe. Historical evidence of their migratory pattern suggests that Ashkenazi Jews represent the 2nd diaspora that occurred during the Jewish-Roman wars around 135 CE when Jews were forbidden to enter Jerusalem. This Jewish group exodus immigrated north to Central and eastern Europe. They ended up in Germany (Germania) and Northern France during the Roman Era (around 800-1000 CE) and were likely merchants that followed the Romans during their conquests. One or several of those Jewish groups included our family. It is within this larger historical and political context that we can begin to situate Poland's role in Ashkenazi Jewish heritage in general and the more local historical and political context of our great grandparents, Sura and Mendel.

Persecution in Europe resulting from the crusades and outbreaks of the plague (of which Jews were blamed), and the Spanish Inquisition in the late 15th century led many Jews to migrate to the Polish Kingdom seeking safety. Before Poland, Jews came from Bohemia (i.e., Czech Republic) and Germany along the Rhine River known as *Ashkenaz*. Jews from this region were recorded as early as A.D. 321. These migrants from Germany and Bohemia are referred to as Ashkenazi Jews and represent the early ancestors of Sura and Mendel. But why, you might be asking, did Ashkenazi Jews head to Poland? Well, that's because Poland needed a workforce to develop their new economy.

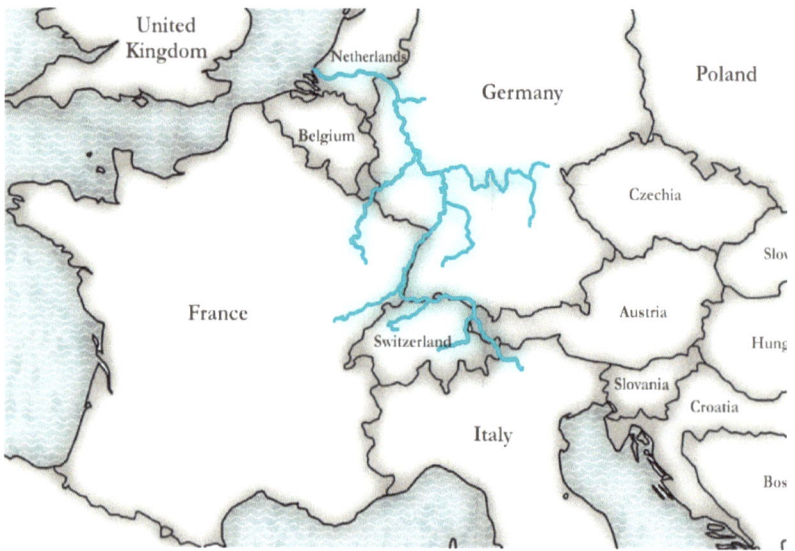

Figure 2: Rhine River, Germany

Taking advantage of the Jewish exodus from Western Europe, Polish kings and the nobility invited Jews to help develop their newly formed Eastern European feudal farm-based economy. This led to Jews playing a unique and pivotal role in developing the Polish-Lithuanian Commonwealth, created in 1569 through a Poland and Lithuania union. Jews provided not only financial services, crafts, and commerce, but estate and farm management labor. Granted exclusive rights over production and tax collection on the private lands of the nobility, Jews were responsible for many aspects of building this feudal economy by helping to manage the estates of the Polish lords, cutting timber, providing raw materials for commerce and collecting taxes and payments from the poor; thereby, serving as the middle managers for the Polish nobility and the poor.

While finding more freedom and security in Poland than in Western Europe, Jews still represented the minority in this new land and continued to experience resentment and hostility as Christians still have significant political power over them. For example, Jews were not allowed to vote, could not hold political office, could not purchase immovable property, could not buy or lease land from peasants, could not employ apprentices or Christian servants, could not participate in peddling, could not live on Warsaw's main streets and were restricted on where they could settle throughout Poland (Polonsky, 2013). The Czarist empire further prohibited Jews from being able to draft documents or wills in Hebrew or Yiddish or from acquiring mines. Jews were levied taxes if they wished to visit Warsaw, taxed on Kosher meat and were taxed for being exempted from serving in military "until they were given full political rights." Even with all this resentment and restrictions, Poland was a safer place to live for Jews than surrounding countries.

Many possible reasons for the antagonism between Jews and the Polish can be extrapolated, including the Jews unwillingness to convert to Christianity, the ever present use of propaganda and military force by Germany and Russia to divide Jews and Poles and weaken Poland, fear or distrust of how weirdly the Jews dressed, the oddness of their Yiddish language, and their incomprehensible customs [3]. Some reasons also connect to how Jews were positioned within the economic structure of Poland at the time. In the feudal period, which lasted until the second half of the 19th century in most of the Polish lands, Jews served as the middlemen between landowners and the poor who labored on the land. For example, Jews were often granted the sole privilege to produce alcohol and run the local bar.[4] A system developed in which Jews helped the landlords to exploit their peasants: collecting grain grown by the poor, making it into alcohol, and selling it back to the peasants, often on credit. The poor resented this process and it was easier to resent Jews than the lords themselves with whom they had no direct contact.

Some of the ways Jews differed from other communities in Poland included in their clothing, food choices, language and names.

Ashkenazi food. As Orthodox Jews[5], Sura and Mendel family likely ate the following foods on the Sabbath, New Moon and annual holidays: wine, matzo soup, challah bread, peppered peas, chopped liver with onions or roasted mutton, sweet noodles, ginger cake, and chicory tea. Everyday food[6] likely consisted of coarse rye bread, potatoes, herring, and beet soup.

Ashkenazi language. Given that Sura and Mendel and their children were Orthodox Jews they likely spoke Yiddish[7] and Polish while growing up in Poland. While the original language of the Jews was Hebrew, it was followed by the Aramaic language (after the Babylonian exile) with Jews picking up linguistic elements of the countries from which they were expelled as they made their way to Poland. *Yiddish* is considered the historical Germanic language of the Ashkenazi Jews. This language began in the 9th century of Central and eastern Europe, and represents a fusion of High German, Hebrew, Aramaic, Slavic and Romance languages. Many Jews could read and write in Hebrew (as required by Orthodox Jews) and spoke a Judeo-German Yiddish dialect (Polonsky, 2013). Sura and Mendel were Orthodox Jews and likely learned and spoke Yiddish and Polish.

Ashkenazi surnames. Ashkenazi Jews did not use surnames before mid 17th century making it near impossible to trace our earlier family lines. Most Christians in Eastern Europe had surnames by the 10th century. As Germans and Eastern Europeans countries wanted to keep track of all their citizens, governments demanded that Ashkenazi Jews choose, or were given, a surname[8] in the late 17th century and early 18th century. Surnames were often chosen based on geographical place or occupation.[9] Our family surnames suggest most surnames were given by occupation. James mother, Sura, family surname *Guteswilen* means rabbi; while her mother's maiden name of *Rubinstejn* means ruby stone cutter; and her paternal grandmother's maiden name *Filut* means flute player. James surname *Rozenwald* means rose woods while his mother's maiden name *Malcman* means beer-maker. Note the origins of our Ashkenazi Jewish family surnames are Germanic and Old French supporting the thesis that Sura and Mendel ancestors arrived in Poland from Germany and Eastern France along with many of the Ashkenazi Jews of the time. These migrants from Germany and Bohemia are referred to as Ashkenazi Jews and represent the early ancestors of Sura and Mendel (See Table 1).

Table 1: Origins of family surnames and likely family relations of Sura Guteswilen and Mendel Rozenwald in Poland before 1910s and after 1920*					
Family Surnames	Polish Towns and Gubernia located**	Origin & meaning of surname***	Total in Poland Before 1910s	Total records in S or M town****	After 1930s*****
GUTESWILEN	Town: **Ciechanow** Gubernia: Plock	Germanic *"God's will"*	61	59	0
MALCMAN	Town: **Siedlce** Gubernias: Lomza, Lublin, Radom, & Warszawa	Germanic *"sickly or malt/beer man"*	459	58	0
FILUT	Town: **Ciechanow**, Gubernias: Krakow, Plock, & Prussia	Old French *"flute"*	305	112	0
ROZENWALD	Town: **Siedlce** Gubernias: Checiny, Kalisz, Kielce, Krakow, Lublin, Lwow, Piotrkow, Radom, Tarnopol, & Warszawa	Germanic Eastern Prussia *"Rosewood"*	1,447	97	2
RUBINSTEJN	In every Polish town	Germanic *"Ruby stone"*	18,071	467	??
		Total	**20,343**	**783**	**2**

*Polish town with largest family surname records & Gubernias (counties) with highest rates (more than 20 records) https://jri-poland.org/juriplweb.htm
**Data from JRI-Poland Records https://jri-poland.org/jriplweb.htm
***Most surnames originated from location or occupation, source https://ancestry.com
****Total in Sura and Mendel birth town https://jri-poland.org/jriplweb.htm
***** Numbers likely result of pogroms, death camps and emigration respectively

Sura Liba Guteswilen Rozenwald

James' mother, SURA LIBA GUTESWILEN, was born in Ciechanow, Poland/Russia in 1877[10]. She was the daughter of Itta RUBINSTEJN and Pinches Guteswilen and had two siblings: Laja and Wolff[11]. Let's explore what life was like for our great grandmother Sura in Ciechanow, Poland circa 1860-1940. Read more about Sura Liba's ancestors in Part II, *Sura and Mendel genealogy family summary.*

According to the *Memorial Book for Ciechanow*[12] (2013), the first recorded Jew in Ciechanow was 1569. Several events happened in the 1600s that may have impacted the ancestors of *Sura Liba Guteswilen* including a huge fire and an epidemic that broke out in the town in 1662 killing many.

Ciechanow is strategically located between the then superpower Russia and the rest of Europe and had been the epicenter for war from its very beginnings. Ciechanow became a town in the early 11th century, shortly after Poland became a country. Attempts to take control over Ciechanow land began as early as 1267 with a war between Lithuania and Prussia. A second war broke out 70 years later between Lithuania and Prussia in 1337 and again approximately 100 years later with the Crusaders in 1460 and then with the Swedes in 1657 and again in the 1700s when Napoleon occupied all of Poland.

Poland Partition 1795-1895

Before WW1, Ciechanow had a thriving Jewish community with famous rabbis, synagogues, schools and community centers. Many from Ciechanow were craftsman and peddlers. During WWI, Russia invaded Poland and life became extremely difficult for all Polish Jews with the Czar's regime and the terror of pogroms. Both the Germans and the Russians hated the Jews. Ciechanow sits close to the German-Russia border, only 100 kilometers from Russia and 40 kilometers to the nearest German village. It's not surprising then to learn that Ciechanow was one of the first towns to fall during WW1. At this time, the Czar ordered that all Jews had to leave Proshnitz which is located 12 kilometers from Ciechanow. It is only a few short years later, approximately 1922, that Sura and Mendel left Poland and ended up in Cuba. Many of Sura's relatives likely did not have the money or means to leave during this volatile period in Poland.

As Germany broke through the Polish front during WW2, Ciechanow holds the sad distinction of being the first Polish town invaded and occupied by Germany. In 1939, Germans completed the Jewish genocide started in WW1 of Ciechanow killing Jews on the spot or sending them to the death camps of Auschwitz and Nurstadt (see Table 1 above). Hated by both the Russians and the Germans and sitting strategically between both superpowers of the time with water to the north and an unfriendly Austria to the south, Polish Jews had little options. Sadly, the USA and England had closed their doors to Jews at this time and secret emigration to Israel was dangerous, costly and rare. There were only a few emigration options at the time for Jews and only those with the money and means could do so: Israel, Canada and Cuba. Thankfully for us, Sura and Mendel had the means and money to travel.

Germans leading Ciechanow Jews to their death, Source: jewgen.org

Germans destroyed many of the Ciechanow synagogues; confiscated property; required all Jews to wear the yellow star and forced them to live in the Jewish Ghetto where poverty, hunger and disease led to many deaths. Elderly Jews were beaten and shot to death. The younger Jews were confined to the Jewish ghettos or were placed on trains and brought to the death camps where they were starved, suffocated, tortured or shot. Sadly, many died in the Jewish Ghettos and death camps. You can find the names of Guteswilen and Rubinstejn Ciechanow relatives in the Jewish (Yizkor) Memorial Holocaust Books.

Initially, Ciechanow was attacked for its strategic location but by the 1500 s war continued to break out due to growing anti-Semitism of the large majority Jewish population located there. For example, check out table 2 below which reveals that by 1802, Jews were the majority ethnic group representing 85% of the total 1,397 inhabitants of Ciechanow. However, a steep decline occurred in the number of Jews living in Ciechanow from a high of 86% in 1880 to a low of 42 % by 1897. The year 1897 is a very significant time for our family as it represents the year following the marriage of Sura Liba Guteswilen and Mendel Rozenwald and when our grandfather, James, was likely born. A few years before James was born, Yassini (2013) reports that there were no Jewish hospitals, orphanages or guest houses left in Ciechanow. Another significant event occurred around this time that likely impacted Sura and Mendel's decision on where to live: A Cholera epidemic. In the first three months of the outbreak, Yassini reports, 90 people died in Ciechanow. Many of the wealthy of the town fled to the city (Warsaw), trade ceased, and rumors spread, as usual, that the Jews were responsible for the epidemic.

Mendel and Sura likely met in the City of Warsaw as many families would bring their trade goods to sell. Sura Liba was born in Ciechanow almost 100 miles from Lukow Poland where Mendel was born. Ciechanow is approximately 47 miles north northwest (52° 53' N 20° 37' E) from the City of Warsaw and Lukow is 63 miles east southeast (51° 55' N 22° 23' E) from Warsaw.

Table 2: Ciechanow Population 1800s*			
Year	General Pop.	Jewish Pop.	% Jewish
1802	1,397	1,194	86
1827	2,640	1,644	62
1860	3,575	2,394	67
1880	5,469	3,761	69
1897	10,000	4,223	42

*Data from *Memorial Book for Jewish Community of Ciechanow*, Yassini, 2013

Mendel Rozenwald

James father, MENDEL ROZENWALD was born in Lukow, located in the Gubernia of Siedlce, Province of Lublin, Poland/Russia on March 25th, 1867. He was the son of Sejzndla MALCMAN and Gerszon Rojzenwald. Note, the not uncommon shifts in spellings of surnames, reflecting the Russian, German, Polish, and Hebrew influences also known as Yiddish.

The province of Siedlce[13] Poland went through many significant upheavals including partitions, incorporations, and liquidations[14] that likely impacted Mendel and his ancestors. At the time of Mendel's birth, the primary occupation in Siedlce was agriculture primarily wheat, barley, rye, oats, potatoes, followed by livestock breeding, with minor manufacturing or trade occurring in Siedlce at this time (Classic Encyclopedia, 1911)[15]. As antisemitism continued to rise, many buildings, homes, synagogues, and hospitals were destroyed leaving very little documentation of the life of Jews in Siedlce.

What is known about Siedlce is that Jews represented approximately 70% (18,000) of the residents during the turn of the 18th century. Yiddish was the more common language heard by Jews in the area although many Jews likely understood and could speak Polish. Most Jews had a difficult time selling their wares as there were no charitable organizations to ameliorate the famine and poverty and no loans available except through extortion. To be a Jew in Siedlce was probably stressful and may be why Mendel likely chose to get married in Ciechanow and live and work in Warsaw.

Siedlce Pogrom: What must have it been like to be a Jew living in Siedlce when the pogrom of 1906 broke out? According to Kopowka, the Siedlce pogrom started when the Russian secret police declared a state of emergency after planning and organizing a massive attack in the hopes of causing enough unrest between the Jews and the Polish that antisemitism would increase, and Poles would want to force out the Jews. Russian soldiers killed 200 , wounded 1000, and arrested more than 3,000 Jews. Jewish-owned stores were robbed, buildings burned, and most homes were destroyed. Historical records describe this 3-day pogrom as an attempt by Russia to exterminate the Jews of Siedlce. The aftermath of this particular pogrom was reported across many major US and Europe papers at the time (see Appendix for news reports from 1906) . The 1906 Siedlce pogrom marks the beginning of mass fear and exodus of Jews from Poland. Political and military pressure from Russia helped to make Poland a less tolerant country for Jews.

Luckily, for us, Sura and Mendel were married in Ciechanow and probably did not live in Siedlce during the 1906 Siedlce pogrom but Mendel's family of origin did. Perhaps, Sura and Mendel were living in Warsaw where at least two of their children were likely born (Itta and Rosa). Warsaw is not far from Siedlce where this brutal pogrom occurred that terrorized and likely killed some of Mendel's family and friends. You can find the names of probable Rozenwald and Malcman Siedlce relatives in the Jewish (Yizkor) Memorial Holocaust Book What happened to Mendel's hometown area? In WW2, as the Germans marched through Poland on their way towards Russia, most of Siedlce was annihilated. Nazis loaded more than 12,500 Jews onto freight cars and sent them to the death camps in Treblinka. It is estimated that 17,000 Jews were murdered from Siedlce during the Nazi occupation. Besides the death camps, the Nazis destroyed every trace of Jewish life in Siedlce burning the synagogues, destroying the cemeteries, building and documents. As a result, sadly, very little documentation exists of this time. The few Jews of Siedlce who escaped went to the US or Israel.

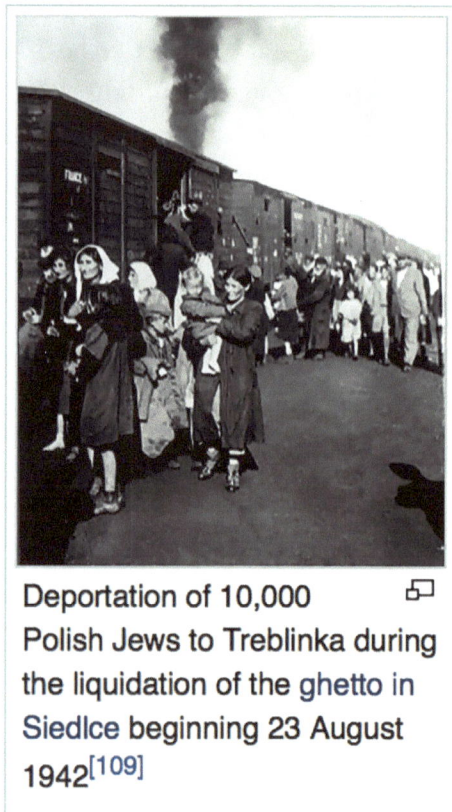

Deportation of 10,000 Polish Jews to Treblinka during the liquidation of the ghetto in Siedlce beginning 23 August 1942[109]

From Wikipedia

Sura and Mendel Rozenwald

Our great grandparents, Sura Liba Guteswilen and Mendel Rozenwald were married[16] on June 18, 1896 in Sura's birthplace of Ciechanow, Poland when Sura was 18 years and Mendel was 20 years of age, suggesting this was a first marriage for both of them. Sura's mother's maiden surname was RUBINSTEJN and Mendel's mother's maiden surname was MALCMAN.

The marriage certificate is written in Yiddish (see Appendix for their marriage certificate and translation extraction).

Sura and Mendel had five children from approximately 1897 through 1912, three boys (James, Adolf and Henry) and two daughters (Itta and Rosa). Given there was no birth control at this time, there were likely miscarriages and/or infant death, but we have no way to confirm. James was likely the oldest sibling followed by Adolf, Itta and Henry. Rosa was the youngest and most of Sura and Mendel's children were likely born in Warsaw, Poland. Unfortunately, almost all Jewish records of that period were destroyed during WW2 by Nazis, so we have no birth records for James and his siblings. James and Adolf were close in age and the boy on the left in the picture below is either James or Adolf. Rosa in the middle is approximately one year old and Itta is approximately 3 years old.

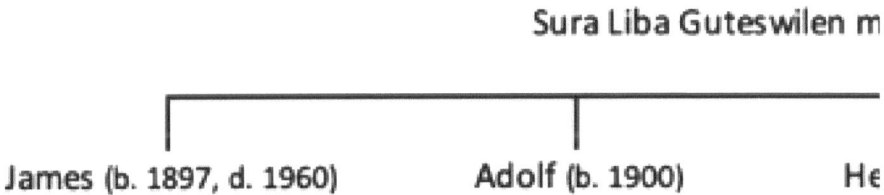

Sura Liba Guteswilen m

James (b. 1897, d. 1960)   Adolf (b. 1900)   He

Ruth Fiche Padoor reported[17] to Debra that James father, Mendel, had been a successful businessman in Poland supplying meat to local businesses— a highly desirable and well-paid occupation. The picture below provides support to Ruth's story of Mendel's success as Sura and her three children are taking a formal photo for the time and are dressed in fine apparel. Many Jews in Poland at the time were peasants and would have been unable to afford a formal photo sitting. Sura's hair and clothing are neatly arranged and everyone appears well fed.

Sura (back) with James or Adolf (L), Rosa (center), and Itta (R) likely Poland, c. 1912

Sura and Mendel leave Poland

Granddaughter Ruth Fisch recalls that Mendel *was a successful business man who sold kosher meat to restaurants and hotels in Poland.* Kosher meat which is created by means of ritual slaughter—involves draining the blood of conscious animals—has been an essential component of the Jewish diet as Jews are forbidden to drink the blood of an animal. Critics[18] of the practice—mainly Christians — sought to ban or limit the ritual practice[19] and the issue became especially heated in 1918 just as Poland was trying recover from WW1 and unite as an independent nation. The tension that rose around the issue of ritual slaughter likely impacted Mendel's kosher meat business negatively and Mendel and Sura likely began to seriously consider leaving the country.

In March 1921, the signing of the *Treaty of Riga* between Russia and Poland marked the end of WW1 for the Poles. Many Poles and Jews thought this would be the beginning of independence as a new democratic constitution was adopted. Sura and Mendel must have believed that things would change for the better as they continued to stay. However, many political factions existed, and politics were volatile as Russia and Germany resented losing control of the Polish land they had obtained during the earlier partitions. The period after WW1 became an extremely stormy time with the possibility of civil war seeming to be close at hand. One year later Mendel and Sura said: "enough."

James parents, Sura and Mendel took their two daughters, Itta and Rosa and left Poland, like thousands of Jews before them, to immigrate to the US. Unfortunately, they waited one year too long to enter the US. Antisemitism and the *KKK* were also rising in the US leading to new US immigration policies between 1921 and 1924 that imposed strict quotas of people from Eastern European countries—places that happened to have the largest Jewish populations. Hence, James family was not allowed to disembark from their boat and instead were sent to Cuba where they eventually settled. When Sura and Mendel landed in Cuba, they arrived with their two younger children, Itta and Rosa. According to James niece, Ruth Fische, Adolf (Abraham) and Henry (Enrique) arrived in Cuba sometime later. Hey, you may ask where the heck was James and his brothers when their parents and sisters left Poland? Why are the Rosenwald boys not with their parents? We address those questions in the next chapter. Before we get there though, let's check out what happened to Sura and Mendel when they arrived in Cuba.

Sura and Mendel lived relatively peacefully in Cuba

When Sura and Mendel arrived in Cuba, they found many other Ashkenazi Jews there, as Cuba was one of the few safe harbors available to escape the growing antisemitism gripping Eastern Europe at the time. While there were some Jews in Cuba[20] before the 1880s, changes to the Cuban constitution in 1902 promoting freedom of religion, suddenly made Cuba an ideal refuge for Eastern European Jews trying to escape the escalating pogroms. Many Jews were seeking to immigrate to the USA, but the stiffening immigration laws prevented this from happening and instead these Jews found themselves settling in Cuba. Sura and Mendel with their two daughters, Itta and Rosa, arrived in Cuba in 1922 at the height of the Jewish immigration wave from Poland to Cuba.

Jews in Cuba. According to Levine,[21] in *Tropical Diaspora: The Jewish experience in Cuba*, Cuba provided more refugee status to Jews than any other Latin American country and proportionally more than the US. Although there was some antisemitism in Cuba, most Jews received a welcome reception from Cubans partly because Jews settled throughout the country avoiding the ghetto situation that often occurred in Europe and because Cuba had an open economy that allowed Jews to take up a variety of jobs. Another reason antisemitism may have been less is that the Cuban elite were well traveled and hence more open to cultural differences. Finally, there were several waves of Jewish migration beginning in the 12th

Century that may have helped each successive Jewish migration assimilate more easily into Cuban society.

Ashkenazi Jews who migrated to Cuba were generally referred to as "Polanco's" who tended to be more orthodox and integrated less easily into Cuban society than the earlier waves of Sephardic Jews. In addition, the Ashkenazi Jews who entered around 1920 and through WW2 viewed Cuba as a "way station" or an "immigration hotel" as they waited to enter the US. The unintended consequence of Ashkenazi Jews aloofness toward Cuba (as they awaited their final journey to the US) might have reduced the antisemitism that often arose in other countries.

According to granddaughter, Ruth Fisch Padoor, *Grandpa Mendel, had been a successful businessman in Poland supplying meat to restaurants and hotels, so he decided to open a little kosher restaurant in Havana. All early Jewish immigrants ate there. My mother and aunt Rose were the waitresses. That is how my parents met, in grandpa Mendel Rosenwald's little restaurant. My father fell in love with my mom and he romanced grandpa first to get his support with mom. Ultimately, grandpa made it happen.*

Below is a photo of Sura and Mendel, likely taken at the same time as the photo in the introduction of this book. Wearing the same clothes as the previous photo but here Mendel is standing with a cane. Sura is a stocky woman and Mendel is not much taller than Sura. They are dressed in fine clothing suggesting they had a successful restaurant business in Cuba.

Sura and Mendel

James' Mother Sura

Below is a photo of Sura with her granddaughter Ruth (Itta's daughter) in Cuba in approximately 1942. Sura looks quite happy and relaxed. This is one of the few photos of Sura smiling. Fanny,[22] Sura's granddaughter (Rosa's daughter) described her grandmother Sura (and her grandfather) as *very loving people.*

Sura with granddaughter Ruth (Itta daughter)

Below is a photo of Mendel with his two daughters Itta and Rosa. In a formal photo shoot, all our dressed up and Mendel is wearing glasses and still appears thin even in his 60s.

Mendel (center sitting) with Itta (L) and Rosa (R) with Itta's husband Abraham Fisch (center back) circa 1930

According to Sura and Mendel's granddaughter Fanny[23] (Rosa's daughter), Mendel suffered from a mental illness[24] and he was involuntarily hospitalized by his daughter Itta in Cuba. Sura could not take care of Mendel and he died shortly after he got into a fight over some cigarettes. During the fight, Mendel was stabbed in the abdomen from which he later died at the age of 77. Sura had a heart murmur, suffered from heart issues[25] and died less than two years after Mendel. According to Fanny, Sura and Mendel were very close and Sura died of a broken heart in 1945 at the age of 73. Both Sura and Mendel are buried in Havana,[26] Cuba very close to each other.[27]

What happened to James and his brothers? As we'll see, most of James life was a thinly veiled deception like his namesake Jacob. In Genesis, Jacob—the farmer—usurped his older brother, Essau—the hunter—not once but twice receiving the coveted blessing from his blind ill failing father Isaac. As a result, Jacob became the father of Abraham—the father of the 12 nations of Jews. The biblical meaning of the name Jacob means *usurper* or *deceiver* since Jacob grabbed the heel (blessing) of his older brother at their birth. For many biblical scholars, Jacob was a "righteous deceiver" as God intended Jacob—the thinker—to usurp his older brother—the brute. In the next chapter, we explore James *righteous deception* as he seeks freedom from the antisemitism and violence spreading throughout Eastern Europe.

---

1. An ancient legend purports that the name Poland derives from two Hebrew words, Po-lin (Here abide), inscribed on a note that descended from heaven and found by Jewish refugees from Germany following the Black Death (ca. 1350 C.E.) and the attendant Jewish massacres. In fact, the earliest known evidence of a Jewish presence on Polish lands, is a description left by a Jewish merchant from Spain in the mid-10th century (Polonsky, 2013).
2. Polonsky, A. 2013. The Jews in Poland and Russia: A Short History. Oxford: The Littman Library of Jewish Civilization.
3. The play Fiddler on the Roof is based on the book by Joseph Stein that was set in the Pale of Settlement of Imperial Russia in 1905, Pale of Settlement represented almost all of Poland conquered by Russia including the birthplaces of James parents. Tevye and his daughters attempts to maintain their Jewish religion while Russia and Christianity expanded across Eastern Europe is the story (e.g., abject poverty, religious customs, language, and dress) of our family and many Eastern European Orthodox Jewish families at that time and place. Source: Wikipedia
4. Jews were less likely to imbibe the alcohol than other peasants due to Jewish customs. Although Jews use wine in religious ceremonies, inebriation is discouraged. For Jews, the Adam and Eve story refers to a grapevine not an apple tree (Jewish Action, 2019). More recent genealogical studies point to a rare gene that discourages alcohol dependence (Genes, Brain and Behavior, 2014).
5. As reported by their granddaughters Fanny and Ruth.
6. Source: http://www.yivoencyclopedia.org/article.aspx/Food_and_Drink
7. This is confirmed by letters written in Yiddish by James and his siblings when they were adults.
8. Jews were required to adopt a surname, have a "useful" occupation (farming or artistry) and to have a permanent residence before they were allowed to receive state permission to marry, Source: Polonsky, 2013 p. 49.
9. Source: Wikipedia and Polonsky (2013)

10. Source: Marriage certificate from JRI-Poland website, Ciechanow records
11. JRI-Poland birth records
12. Memorial (Yizkor) Book for the Jewish Community of Ciechanow Ed by A. Wolf Yassini 2013. NY: JewishGen, Inc.
13. Source: The Jews in Siedlce 1850-1945, by Edward Kopowka 2014. NY: JewishGen, Inc. According to Kowpowka (2014), Siedlce, Poland has many meanings including "Shed lets." Shed meaning devil and lets meaning jester give the Jewish meaning "evil spirit". Given the bad luck to those that lived in Siedlce, this name seems sadly fitting. Siedlce sits very close to the border of Russia, is the third largest province of Poland, and had one of the largest Jewish populations outside of Warsaw. Hence, it is perhaps not surprising that Siedlce was targeted by the Russian and the Germans in WW1 and WW2, respectively.
14. Upheavals included:

   • Siedlce was first mentioned in 1448, and Jews are first mentioned in a charter granted by Wladyslaw IV on Dec 1634.
   • In 1730, there were only 29 Jewish families listed in property inventories and approximately 375 Jewish families are mentioned in property inventories in 1794.
   • After the partition of 1804, Siedlce, Poland became part of Austria.
   • After the war of 1809, Siedlce became incorporated into the Duchy of Warsaw.
   • In 1815 after the creation of the kingdom of Poland, Siedlce becomes the city of Podlasie Province
   • which shortly later (1845) was liquidated to become Siedlce District of Lublin Province.
   • In 1867-1912, Siedlce became the provincial seat of newly created Siedlce Province.

15. Classic Encyclopedia 1911 https://encyclopedia.jrank.org
16. Sura and Mendel marriage certificate, located in JRI-Poland records for
17. Ciechanow Plock Gubernia, (records in Fond 572 Warszawa Archive Mlawa Branch), Located at 52°53' 20°37'
18. email correspondence in 2018
19. Critics of the practice represent some of the earliest animal welfare movements in Europe. Plach, E. 2014. Ritual slaughter and animal welfare in interwar Poland. Eastern European Jewish Affairs, 45:1, 1-25
20. Christians argued that the practice was unusually cruel to the animal and instead stun the animal from consciousness during the bloodletting. Polonsky, 2103
21. Source: https://www.jewishvirtuallibrary.org/cuba-virtual-jewish-history-tour
22. Levine, R. M. 2010. Tropical Diaspora: The Jewish experience in Cuba.
23. Debra interviewed Fanny through her son Salomon by phone in February 24, 2019. Salomon translated as Fanny spoke Spanish. Fanny was in a Miami nursing home at the time.
24. Phone interview, see above.

25. Fanny's description of Mendel's symptoms sounded like he suffered from dementia or Alzheimer's per Fanny's son, medical doctor, Salomon Imiak and to Debra Harkins, a clinical psychologist.
26. Heart disease is a very common cause of death in our Rozenwald family. Sura's heart disease suggests that the heart issues may have originated from the Guteswilen line. Check out Rozenwald heart disease incidences chart in Part 2.
27. Mendel's burial location, Havana, Cuba, Plot located on Street E. Block 5 , Grave #18 Sura Liba's burial location, Havana, Cuba, Plot located on Block 3 , Grave #4
28. As of March 2019, Sura and Mendel had 5 children, 20 known grandchildren, 27 known great grandchildren and more than 50 great great grandchildren.

2

CROSSES BORDER TO UK

Jacob went to his father and said, "My father." "Yes, my son," he answered. "Who is it?"

Jacob said to his father, "I am Esau your firstborn. Then Isaac said to Jacob, "Come near so I can touch you, my son, to know whether you really are my son Esau or not. "Jacob went close to his father Isaac, who touched him and said, "The voice is the voice of Jacob, but the hands are the hands of Esau." "Are you really my son Esau?" he asked. "I am," he replied.

Isaac said, "Then I will bless you."

— GENESIS, 27

When Sura and Mendel left Poland in 1922 with their two young daughters, Itta and Rosa, James was approximately 26 years old, his brother Adolf approximately 20 years old and his youngest brother Henry was about 16 years old. By this time, James had already served in WW1 for the British and was married with two children (Bernard and Hetty). So, you may ask, as we did, when did James and his brothers leave Poland? We had to work backwards to make sense of this so bear with us as we describe how we figured out when James, and his brothers, likely crossed the border and why they did so "under cover."

James daughter, Sylvia recalled[1] her father telling her that he began living with his uncle in London, England when he was 11 years old; while, his 2nd wife Caroline remembered[2] James telling her that he began living with his uncle when he was 9 years old. James told his daughter that he sat close to the fire where he learned more languages—eventually learning to speak five languages. Learning English was the fastest and most advantageous way for immigrants to become angelized and obtain a job.

Like most Eastern European Jews, James likely spoke only Yiddish and Polish when he arrived in England and had to change his clothes and language to more easily fit in in his new home. In Poland, James had been educated in a one room schoolhouse in Eastern Europe with a focus on the Bible, prayer and other religious materials along with some writing and math all learned in Yiddish. According to Gartner, more than 90% of Jewish immigrants who came from Eastern Europe did not attend secondary school in England. Most boys left school by 13 or 14 years of age and left their Jewish studies by the age of 13. At this point, many boys began an apprenticeship while some attended evening classes. Tailors did not require an apprenticeship and began working as "learners" for minimum wage until they learned the trade.

James also told Sylvia that his uncle had been abusive to him. James likely sat by the fire to read because no other light was available in the squalor living conditions in poverty-stricken Whitechapel, representing one of the few Jewish communities in England at the time. Lying about his age, itching to get into the fight that was causing so much suffering to his immediate family and trying to escape the poverty and his uncle's abuse, James enlisted in the military in 1914 at the start of WW1 when he was approximately 16years-old. We will discuss what we learned of James time in the military shortly; but first, we want to continue to work backwards to explain how James likely got into England in the first place.

From Poland to England

So, while James parents and sisters left Poland in 1922, James likely left in approximately 1907-1909 when he was between 9 and 11 years of age. Recall from Chapter one, that a terrifying pogrom occurred in 1906 in Siedlce, Poland, the likely birthplace of James father's Mendel, terrifying the Ashkenazi Jews enough that many fled. In addition, the revolution of 1905-1907 led to more social and political violence and pogroms as the tsarist empire attempted to severely oppress revolutionary forces. The Tsar also officially stopped Jewish emigration from Eastern Europe. James parents were likely looking for a way to protect their children from the everincreasing violence spreading across Poland.

Unfortunately, Europe had also begun to close its doors to Eastern European Jews during this time. In England for example, this unwelcome stance occurred with some of the first ever immigration laws passed in Parliamentary legislation through *The Aliens Act of 1905*[3] which specifically focused on restricting Jewish immigration from Eastern Europe.[4] Although Sura and Mendel may have had the financial resources to leave Poland and relatives living in England who could sponsor them, *the Aliens Act* closed the door for Eastern Europeans to enter England *legally.*

A GREAT
PUBLIC DEMONSTRATION
Under the auspices of
THE BRITISH BROTHERS' LEAGUE,
in favour of restricting the further immigration o
DESTITUTE FOREIGNERS
into this Country, will be held at
THE PEOPLE'S PALACE,
MILE END, E., on
TUESDAY, JAN. 14TH, 1902.

The Chair will be taken at Eight p.m. sharp, by
MAJOR EVANS-GORDON, M.P.,
who will be supported by Members of Parliament, County and Borough Councillors, Members of Boards of Guardians of all shades of politics, and Ministers of Religion of all Denominations.

Source: Google

At first, Britain were sympathetic to the plight of Jews who were suffering under the repressive regime of the Russian Tsar. Unfortunately, the initial enthusiasm waned when thousands of Jews began to emigrate into London and surrounding towns. Even before the Alien Act, Britain and English Jews tried to dissuade Eastern Europeans from emigrating to England writing in newspapers and sending letters to Jews in Eastern Europe suggesting not to come; writing that the English natives were bitter to immigrants, that they make you shave your beard, and that they try to dilute Judaism.[5] These scare tactics had little impact on the oppressed and povertystricken Jews suffering in Eastern Europe and more than 120,000 Jews came to England between 1870-1914.

James (and his brother Adolf) likely illegally entered England sometime between 1907-1909 (no records exist for Jacob Rozenwald, James Rosen or James Rosenwald in Poland or England until 1915), 5 years after Britain put immigration restrictions into place to stop the influx of Jews from Eastern Europe. The *British Brothers League,* a **nationalist** organization, was created around the turn of the century that organized, marched and held rallies supporting anti-immigration policies. At their rallies, speakers argued that Britain *should not be the dumping ground for the scum of Europe*. Newspapers continued with similar propaganda with the *Manchester Evening Chronicle* in 1905 writing *that the dirty, destitute, diseased, verminous and criminal foreigner who dumps himself on our soil and rates simultaneously, shall be forbidden to land*. At this time, Britain passed *The Aliens Act* of 1905, which ostensibly was to prevent criminals and paupers from entering the country, but the Act's main objective was to keep Jews from Eastern Europe out of England. As immigration restrictions were still loosely enforced from Europe, people could get into England by many means including hiding in the back of a truck, on hiding on a ship or hidden under some blankets on a carriage. It is likely that a family member "smuggled" James (and perhaps Adolf) into Britain to escape the ever-worsening anti-Semitic conditions in Poland that preceded the outbreak of WW1 in 1914. Given that Henry was much younger than James or Adolf, his parents likely sent Henry out of Poland much later. No naturalization papers have been found for James or his brothers in England supporting the hypothesis that James had no ID papers to begin the naturalization process. James, like many Jews trying to escape the growing antisemitism in Eastern Europe, was hiding in Britain as an illegal alien.

How did Jews get into England when the Russian Tsar had made it illegal to leave Eastern Europe and when England had closed its doors to Jews? There were three steps needed to make this emigration journey[6]; first they needed to have the money and means to get to the seaport; second, they needed to have the money to travel by sea; and third, they needed to have help when they debarked into England. At each point on this journey troubles ensued and significant money was needed to pay for each leg of the journey including for the train ride to the seaport; to pay for the ship; to pay Russian officials and emigration agents to be "blind" to the illegal exodus; and to have someone help them when they arrived in England. Very few Jews were able to secure a passport; only a few were able to pay for "fake" passports; most Jews had no passports and hid as stowaways in cargo ships. Most of these emigrations took place on ships setting sail to England from Germany: Rotterdam, Libau, Bremen and Hamburg. To get to these German seaports, Jews took a train from their Polish towns. The main ports where Jews debarked in England included Grimsby, Glasgow, Harwich and London.

The 3-day cargo voyage from Germany to England[7] usually meant Jews had only the food they were able to carry on board (usually potatoes and herring) and this meant sleeping in the hull of the cargo ship. Many Jews arrived in England hungry and disheveled. Once landed, if they were lucky, relatives picked them up. Unfortunately, for many of these immigrants, thieves and sharks were ready to take advantage of those without family including pimps who preyed on young girls and quickly sent them into brothels, as well as thieves— who spoke Yiddish—who convinced many that they would help them only to steal their money and meager supplies. In London, most newly arrived Jews went to the *Poor Jews' Temporary Shelter* for a maximum of 14 days for single men and try to help them find a place to live. More than 95% of these Jews went on to the US[8]. Those Jews that stayed often had relatives living in England. Most of these Eastern European Jews went to London specifically the East End, Spitalfields area where many earlier Jewish immigrants were located, and where work and housing could be found.

There were at least two major reasons James parents sought to get James and his brother Adolf out of Poland in the first decade of the 1900s including the Revolution of 1905 and the pogroms that followed. Fortunately, the *Atlantic Shipping Ring* dissolved[9] around this time and a price war began on the high seas. The dissolution of this shipping policy meant that shippers would now sell tickets to those trying to emigrate out of Eastern Europe and because of the price wars, travel prices dropped enough for many Jews to be able to afford to leave. The highest number of Jewish immigrants to England occurred between 1905-1906.

James illegal entry into Britain helps to explain what Jimmy and I discovered early on in our genealogy search. James shortened his surname from Rozenwald to Rosen in his teens (at least by 1915 when he was approximately 15-16 years old) and used the anglicized version of his given name. So, Jacob became James. His military records list James as Jim Rosen, even though the rest of his family kept the full surname of Rosenwald when they immigrated to Cuba. Many Eastern Europeans who immigrated to England during this time period anglicized their German-sounding given names and surnames to stand out less in an antisemitic climate. James parents and sisters who immigrated to Cuba arrived in a slightly more welcoming country and likely did not feel the need to change their surname.

British Military Service

We know James served in WW1 from family photos (see below), military records[10] and family lore. James, who identified as Jim during his time in the military, was barely 16-years-old when he enlisted. He was of small stature with a bit of a lost look when he first entered the service.

James Rosen, circa 1916 WW1 British military

James served in WW1 in the *Royal Army Service Corp* (RASC) which was the transport division of the British military. These RASC soldiers provided the mechanical transport of supplies to the armies. There were two means of RASC transport; automobile and horse transport. As James military ID has a T prefix,[11] he was part of the horse transport corps division that transported provisions to all other army units using horse drawn wagons (see image below).

IWM image Q4831. Horse wagons of the Army Service Corps at a roadside dump for supplies. Albert, Somme, March 1917. From https://www.longlongtrail.co.uk/army/regiments-and-corps/the-army-service-corps-in-the-firstworld-war/

In the photo below, James appears to be in his "dressed down" uniform probably due to the heat while serving for the British in Africa. The back of the photo, written in his second wife's, Caroline, handwriting, says *1914-1916*. Many Jews served in theatres of war like Palestine and Egypt and James likely served in Egypt. Sylvia recalls her father, James, telling her that while he was a soldier and in Africa he was attacked by knife. She describes seeing her father's back covered in deep scars and James telling her at the time that the scars were from the war. This is likely why James received a Victory Medal and the British War Medal (See Appendix for images of medal records).

James circa 1920s

After 1920 when James finished his six years of active duty in the RASC, James was remobilized for another 5 years into the Army Reserve serving for a total of 11 years. Approximately 60% of the first world war British Army soldiers service records[12] were tragically damaged or destroyed due to enemy bombing in 1940. The 2 ,000 surviving "burnt records" represent soldiers who were killed, demobilized, or discharged between 1914 and 1920. Luckily James military records survived the bombing. Unfortunately, this is not true for the military records of his younger brother Adolf.

James younger brother, Adolf likely served in the first world war too, but he did not discharge his service and hence his military records represent some of those destroyed in 1940. Adolf first appeared in ship manifest records beginning at the end of the second world war in 1945 where he was traveling from Cuba to Florida. Adolf is easily traceable through multiple ship manifests thereafter too. His absence from all records before 1945; his absence when his parents emigrated out of Poland; and the destruction of much of the UK first world war military records lends support to our thesis that Adolf served in both world wars and probably between the wars. When Adolf finally joined his family in Cuba after the war, he like his parents, sisters, and younger brother made Cuba his permanent residence. That is, until 1966 when he became a naturalized citizen of the US. See photos and read more about Adolf in Part II, *Adolfo genealogy family summary.*

James youngest brother, Henry, who would have been too young to serve in the first world war likely served in the second world war. Similar to Adolf, Henry, was not found in any documents before the two world wars. Given Henry was about 16 years old when his parents left Cuba in 1922, he may have been sent to England as an "apprentice" where James was living. After Henry's probable service in the second world war, he eventually made his way to his family in Cuba and lived there for many years before moving permanently to Miami, Florida. See photo and read more about Henry in Part II, *Henry genealogy family summary.*

James likely spent much of his early life hiding in plain sight—like many Jews at the time—from the rampant antisemitism that gripped much of Eastern and Western Europe. Lipman (1990) writes that open antisemitism occurred in Britain following the Russian Revolution and the period of 1917-1921 creating much anxiety for British Jews. Hence, it is not surprising then that while James felt relatively safe in England from the violence and pogroms of Eastern Europe, James kept his real name— Avraham Yankel (Jacob) Rozenwald—and birthplace hidden for many years likely still justifiably fearful of the open antisemitism in England. In our next chapter, we explore James life in England before he headed to America.

1. Interview with Sylvia in January 2019 with daughter Debra
2. Interview with Caroline in 1985 with granddaughter Debra
3. The Aliens Act of 1905 stayed in place until 1914 (start of WW1) when it became even more restrictive. The Act was repealed in 1919.
4. A significant increase in Eastern European Jews occurred in the 1880s setting the stage for the creation of the Aliens Act of 1905.
5. Gartner, 1976. Jewish Immigrant in England, 1870-1914.
6. ibid Gartner, 1976
7. Liepman, 1990. Steamers from Hamburg, Rotterdam, Breman, and Libau traveled weekly to London.
8. Liepman, 1990. Many went thru England at the time because The British Lines were competing for customers and it was cheaper to travel from Eastern Europe to England than straight to US.
9. ibid Gartner, 1976
10. Military records of James Rosen, WW1 British Jewry Book of Honor, 154678 Pnr, 4th Spec Bn
11. A prefix of "T" before a soldier number indicate horse transport Source:
12. www.longlongtrail.co.uk/army/regiments-and-corps/the-army-service-corps-inthe-first-world-war/
13. http://www.greatwar.co.uk/research/military-records/british-soldiers-ww1service-records.htm

3

MARRIES, FATHERS AND WORKS

And God blessed Noah and his sons, and said unto them, be fruitful, and multiply, and replenish the earth…

— -GENESIS, 9:1,7

James and Sarah marriage[1]

In 1918 at the end of WW1, James married his first wife Sarah Reubens. Note, in their wedding picture below, James is approximately 21 years old and Sarah is about 25 years old. James identified himself as James Rosen on his marriage certificate to Sarah and lied about his father's name listing him as Solomon. James was likely still fearful of the ever-present antisemitism and was still trying to stay "under cover." As James was still in the Army at the time, he is wearing his military uniform and looking quite handsome and happy while Sarah is wearing glasses, a simple dress and appears somber.

As mentioned in the introduction, James not only used the Anglicized version of his real given name—Jacob—on his first marriage certificate (1918) but he used the shortened anglicized version of his surname Rosen rather than Rozenwald. James also misidentified his father as Solomon Rosen. He likely did so to protect himself and perhaps his parents from the antisemitism that might have resulted from correctly identifying his father as Mendel Rozenwald from Poland. To be sure to keep others off his trail, James listed his father's occupation as a commercial traveler rather than the real job he held in Poland at the time which was a kosher meat purveyor.

James Rosen and first wife Sarah Reuben wedding picture

In 1920 James was living in a flat in the Jewish section of London on 123 Arlington Road, Camden[2] (see image below from Google maps of where James and Sarah lived) with Walter Alibrow and Joseph Sutherland, likely military buddies. Sarah does not show up on the electoral record rolls until 1925, seven years after women received the right to vote in England. Sarah was likely living with James beginning in 1918 at 123 Arlington suggesting that at least four adults and two of their oldest children (Bernard and Hetty) were living at this address from 1920-1922. Walter and Joseph had left by 1923; but James stayed with Sarah and their two oldest children—Bernard and Hetty.

123 Arlington Rd, Camden, London, England (flats where James and
Sarah lived still standing as of 2019)

Jewish housing sections of England tended to be in the East End of London (e.g., Whitechapel, St. George-in the East, Spitalfield, Leylands in Leeds, and Mile End Old Town) that were often rundown and expensive[3]. Flats were often small, dank and dirty without heat, flushing water or electricity. Sanitary issues were severe in these often overcrowded, poorly built houses[4]. It was not uncommon for Jews to live with up to eight people in a two-room flat[5]. Many of these two room flats shared a toilet and kitchen with the adjacent flat. Eastern European Jews who had recently immigrated to London had lived in small towns in their home country and lacked an understanding of urban sanitation, garbage collection, or sewage disposal[6]. Similarly, many immigrants would close up their fireplaces creating a cinder-filled space with little fresh air.

When James and Sarah first moved to Arlington Road, this area was primarily a Jewish neighborhood with a mix of middle class, poor and extreme poverty as can be seen in one of the famous London poverty maps created by sociologist Charles Booth from 1905. Note, the blue dot below for 123 Arlington Road has dark blue colors nearby that indicate extreme poverty[7].

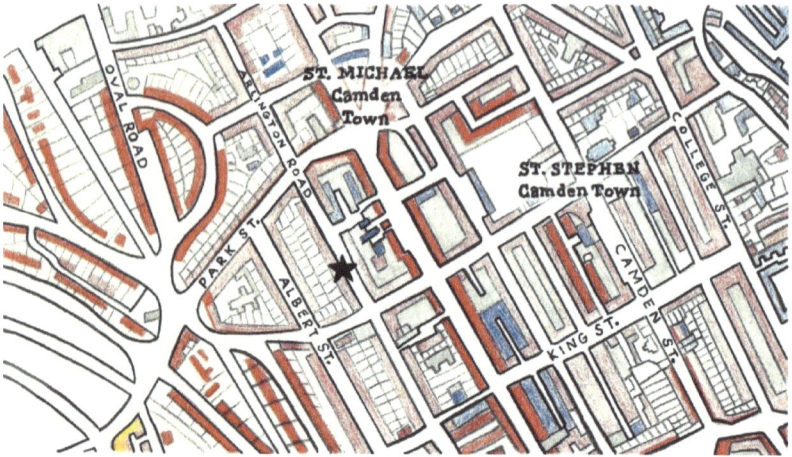

123 Arlington Rd, 1905, from Charles Booth London poverty maps. Note, dark colors (black, green and bluish) indicate extreme poverty, pink colors indicate mixed middle and poor.

Britain social context[8]

Between the two world wars, 1918-1939, British Jews had three big challenges: 1) how to react to Zionism and the possibility of a new Jewish national home; 2) continued anti-Semitism and how to react to rising British fascism; and 3) how to react to the incoming refugees from Central Europe. Although we do not know what James thought or spoke about these issues, he would have at least been indirectly impacted especially regarding his own citizenship question. At the end of WW1, the backlog for Eastern Europeans to become permanent residents in Britain skyrocketed to 22 years. This may be why there is no naturalization record of James ever becoming a British citizen. The cost to naturalize was also prohibitive for many of the working-class Jewish immigrants in Britain effectively delaying or denying British citizenship to Eastern Europeans. From 1932 on, acts of vandalism to synagogues, physical violence and bricks thrown thru Jewish homes rose in East London as economic depression hit Britain hard. By 1934, fascists (British Union of Fascists or BUF) were marching through the heavily Jewish populated areas of East End London in black shirts with Nazi bands and flags.

The *Jewish Labour Council* founded the *Jewish People's Council* representing the Trade Unions and Worker's circle in an attempt to unite Jews against the relentless fascist and antisemitic attacks. Sadly, the police and authorities were doing little to help calm the situation and in too many instances ignored the fascist provocations and violence. In 1933, when Hitler took power, a national boycott of Jewish businesses began, and the first anti-Jewish legislation took hold. By 1935, Jews were denied citizenship. As WW2 erupted, Jewish children and pregnant mothers were evacuated from London to the countryside. The side effect of these evacuations is that many children were no longer exposed to traditional Jewish settings accelerating their anglicization. One example is that the speaking, writing and reading of Yiddish died out within a generation.

James the tailor

James was a master tailor for women's clothing. His occupation is not surprising given tailoring was the number one occupation for most Jews when they arrived in England. There are several reasons why tailoring became the most common Jewish occupation including: 1) that most of the gilded trades were not open to newly arrived Jews; 2) at least a quarter of Jews had made garments before their arrival in England; 3) it was economically feasible to purchase a sewing machine and become an employer[9]; 4) most larger companies required working on Saturdays and Jews did not want to work on the Sabbath; and 5) tailoring was more easily learned compared to other vocational skills like printing and cabinet making. Tailoring[10] was the most popular Jewish immigrant trade at the time in England, Canada, United States, and France and Jews had this trade sewed up (silly pun intended). However, the workshops were often located in homes with up to five workers in small, dark, dank quarters and many business owners (including Jewish owned workshops) still forced the new Jewish immigrants to work on the Sabbath.

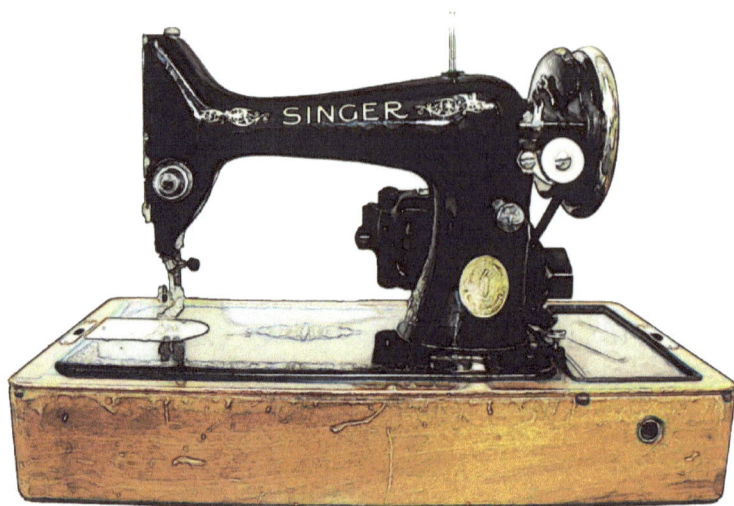

Singer sewing machine, circa 1920s

One of the significant challenges for Jews in the East End was that many workshops were located in homes making it difficult to keep their homes clean. Tailoring, boot and shoe making were particularly unhealthy occupations with the tanning materials and constant bending position involved creating malformations of the vertebrae and pelvis (stooping and pallor), swelling and tumors of the veins, femur and legs, miscarriages, menstruation and skin disorders. Working and living in crammed, lint-filled, unhygienic, smoky spaces without sanitary facilities created a breeding ground for lung diseases like tuberculosis. More than 65% of those that succumbed to the TB epidemic in London during this period were Jewish tailors, furriers, boot and shoe makers, cap makers and cigarette makers[11]. Jimmy recalls his mother Eva (James and Sarah's 2nd daughter) describing the home where she grew up as being dark with a dirt floor characteristic of many East Ender Jewish homes during this period. Although master tailors made only slightly more than their workers, some, like James, were able to eke out a working class or lower-middle class lifestyle. [12]

Workers in East End London circa 1900s

James mystery

The following photo was found in the personal belongings of James 2nd wife Caroline where she wrote on the back: "*Dad and his brother*." James niece, Ruth Padorr confirmed that this photo was Adolf. Caroline did not read Yiddish, so she likely did not know what it said nor that this was Adolf. Sylvia did not know that James had been in contact with any of his siblings while in London.

Adolf endearingly writes to his mother, *my very beloved and forever dear Mama'lah,* and tells her that *you should live* as he has found his *beloved brother, Avraham Yankel.* Adolf tells his mother that James *is with me here in London.* Adolf signs endearingly with his Yiddish name *Your beloved son Itche Lieb.* Perhaps Adolf was asked by his parents to find James and he did. James mother may have been distraught at not knowing where to find her son James. Adolf seems a bit surprised to find James when he states: "*Imagine, my brother.*" And he seems further surprised that he found James in London suggesting that his parents and siblings did not know that James was living in London. How did James become lost and for how long? How did Adolf know how to find James? Did James share this news with either of his wives? Why did James not share this news with his children? This remains a mystery.

Another shroud around this photo is that it is actually a postcard that was never mailed. Why? Did Adolf leave it in London when he went back to Cuba? Why did James have this postcard? Did someone give this postcard to James when he went to Cuba? What seems clear is that this postcard was meaningful to James as he kept it with his belongings that Caroline eventually inherited.

Brothers Adolfo (L) and James (R)

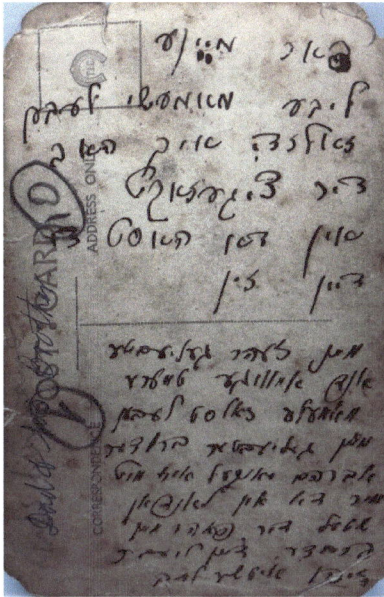

On backside of photo of James and Adolf

My very beloved and forever dear Mama'leh, you should live, my beloved brother Avraham Yanke is with me, here in London. Imagine, my brother. Your beloved son Itche Leib.

— YIDDISH TRANSLATION

James Domestic Life[13]

The complexities of immigration often strained immigrant families. Uncles often replaced fathers and cousins replaced siblings as these newly arrived Jews sought social support. Many Eastern European Jews avoided speaking their native Yiddish and Polish and changed their clothing and hairstyles in an attempt to appear more anglicized. They brought with them more traditional ideas including having many children. Sadly, most people of this period did not speak about, much less understand, the impact that immigration could have on family dynamics.

Before 1922, the national average for number of children was 2.5 and after 2.2, while Jewish women before 1922 had on average 4.0 children and after 1922 the rate was 2.0. James and his first wife Sarah had six children while living on Arlington Road; that is, until Sarah tragically died of heart failure during an operation to fix a uterine prolapse in April of 1937. She was only 41 years of age and left James and their six children: 18-year-old Bernard, 16-year-old Hetty, 13-year-old Eva, 10-year-old William, 8-year-old Stanley, and 2-year-old Reginald. Sarah's death along with James early separation from his parents and siblings, the challenges of immigration and the abusive life he suffered from his uncle, likely made it close to inevitable that James would have volatile relationships with most of his seven children. The volatility with his children began with his first son Bernard (Bunny).

Bernard Rosen. James first son, Bunny[14] was born in 1919 in Marylebone, England. James went into business (type unknown) with his oldest son Bunny. Unfortunately, James and Bunny had a fight about the business and in 1948 bankruptcy ensued[15] and James and Bunny likely never spoke again. Similar to James, Bunny suffered from heart disease[16] and died at the young age of 65.

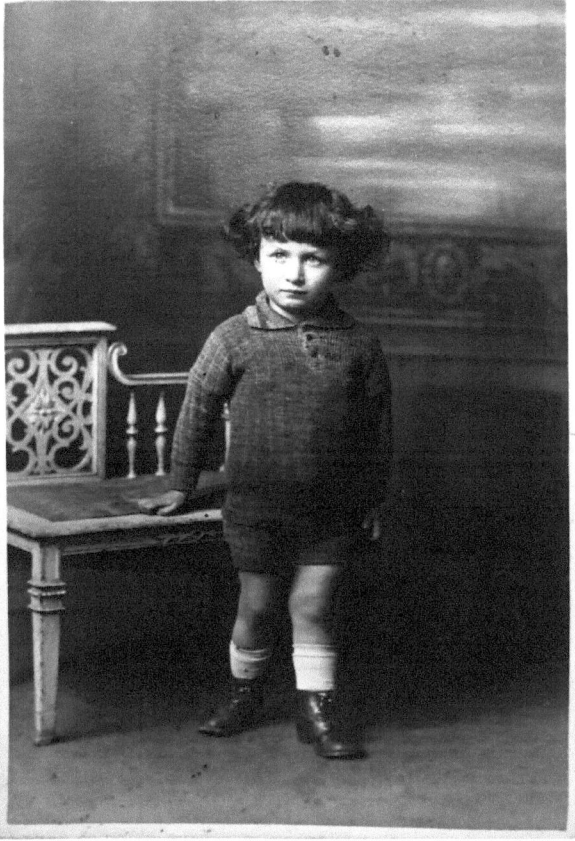

Bernard, approximately 5 years of age, circa 1920's

Hetty Rosen. James relationship with his oldest daughter Hetty (Helen) was also volatile but for a different reason. Helen was born 2 years after her oldest brother Bunny in 1921 in London. Helen lost her mom at the age of 16 and had her first child, Cecilia Rosen in 1940 at the age of 19. Her daughter Cecilia was born with Down's syndrome and died at the age of 3, one year after Helen married William Maddock. Helen and Bill had one daughter; Carol who was born in 1944 while still living in England. Helen, Bill and Carol moved to Canada and Helen likely never spoke to James again.

Helen (r) with husband Bill and daughter Carol

Eva Rosen. James second daughter, Eva was born in London in 1924, three years younger than her older sister Helen. Eve was only 13 years old when she lost her mother. Eve ran away several times after losing her mother. She enlisted in the military five years later in 1942 at the age of 18 and served until 1946. Eve married one year later in England and moved to the US in 1950. After the sudden death of her husband, Harry, when her daughter, Susan, was only one year old, Eve asked James to move to the US, which he did with his 2nd wife Caroline, his youngest children Reggie and Sylvia in 1951. James moved his family in with his daughter Eve in Lawrence, MA. Like all the volatile relationships he had with his children, James got into a fight with Eve (unknown what this fight was about) and James stormed out with his wife and youngest daughter and moved to Dorchester, MA. Eve later married again and had one child, Mark. Like many from the Rosen tribe, Eve died of heart failure; fortunately, at the ripe old age of 77.

Eva circa 1940's

William Rosen, James second son, was born in London in 1927. Billy was only 10 years old when his mother died. James youngest daughter Sylvia does not remember her brother Billy living with the family when she returned in 1946 after their WW2 evacuation. Sylvia[17] stated that she did not meet Billy until he came to the US in 1963 when he was about 36 years of age. Billy is believed to have married and was arrested in NY for passing bad checks and sent back to the UK. Sadly, it is unclear if James or anyone in Billy's immediate family was in touch with Billy after his mother died. No one remembers Billy before or after 1963.

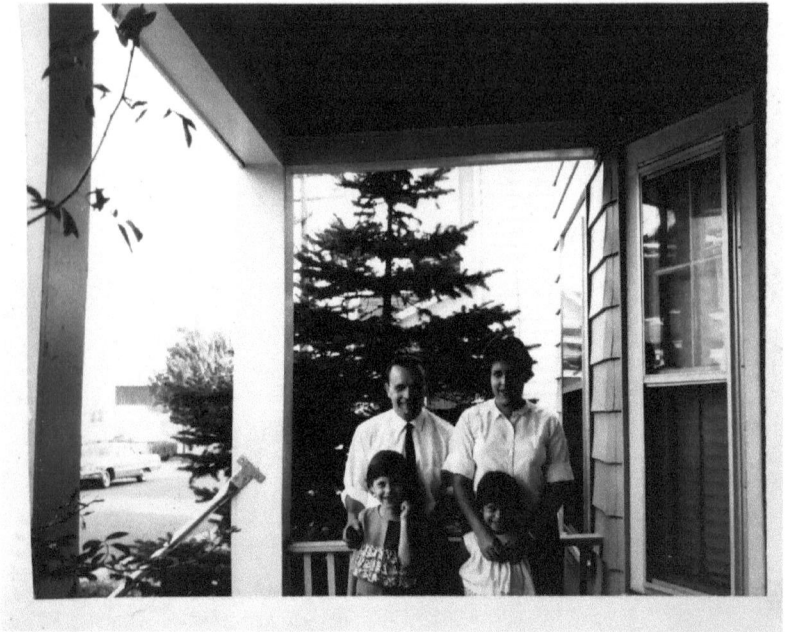

Billy with sister Sylvia and nieces Debra (l) and Marsha (r)

Stanley Douglas Edwin Rosen, James third son, was born in London in 1929
. Three months after the death of his mother Sarah, James, sent 8- year-old
Stanley to live with Sarah's brother Arthur Reubens and wife Mariam in
Toronto, Canada in 1937. James youngest daughter Sylvia remembers her
brother Stanley saying he would never marry due to the physical and
emotional abuse he suffered from his Uncle Art and Aunt Mariam and he
never did. Perhaps, because Stanley felt slighted by James and/or wished to
honor his uncle Art and/or honor his mother, he changed his named to
Arthur Stanley Reubens at the age of 22, on September 26, 1951, days
before he arrived in Buffalo, NY from Canada. Shortly thereafter, Stanley
began living with his sister Eve. Sylvia remembers meeting Stanley for the
first time in 1953 when she was 12 years old in her Cambridge home. She
remembers that she thought he looked like a famous and goodlooking movie
star of the time.

Sadly, like with most of his children James did not seem to maintain a relationship with his third son Stanley upon his arrival to the US. Stanley served from 1953 to 1955 as a Corporal in the US Army. Upon discharge from the Korean war, he moved back to his sister Eve's home in Cambridge Mass. Stanley worked with his sister Eve's second husband until his death. Like most of the Rosen men, Stanley died of heart failure at the young age of 46 and is buried at Temple Emanuel in Andover, MA with his sister Eve.

Stanley with niece Marsha

Reginald Leslie Rosen, James fourth and youngest son, was born in London in 1935. Probably most impacted by losing his mother when he was only 2 years old, Reggie had a turbulent life and it does not appear that James, who was probably traumatized himself, was particularly empathetic. Reginald (Reggie), like many London children during WWII was evacuated to the English countryside from 6-11 years of age and suffered from allergies and asthma while he lived on the farm. After the war, 16-year-old Reggie was brought to the US with James, his stepmother, Caroline, and half-sister, 10year-old Sylvia in 1951. A year later in 1952, Reggie's father and sister Eve had a big fight that led to James, stepmother, and halfsister moving to Dorchester, MA. However, 17-year-old Reggie decided he did not want to live with James anymore and continued to live with his sister Eve in Lawrence.

At age 18, Reginald joined the US selective service in 1953 while he lived in Cambridge, MA. Reggie had a gambling problem which may have contributed to his attempted suicide sometime between 1963 and 1965 (3-5 years after James died) with sleeping pills, while living with his stepmother, Caroline. At age 31, Reggie married and had one child. Sadly, Reggie died from an overdose of pills at the age of 36 and is buried at Askenaz Cemetery in Everett, MA with his father and stepmother.

James Rosen 3rd and 4th sons respectively, Reggie (L) and Stanley (R)

By 1939, two years after James first wife, Sarah Rosen died, James is found on the registrars living at 3 Fairmead Road in Islington, London likely with three of his children[18]. This area of London, according to Charles Booth poverty maps from 1900s, was a mixed community of comfortable and poor Jews.

3 Fairmead Road, Islington, London (where James lived in 1939)

James and Caroline marriage

Two years after the death of his first wife Sarah, James[19] married Caroline Franks in London England in 1939. On their marriage certificate[20], for the first time James lists himself as Jacob Rosen and his father as Mendel suggesting he finally felt safer than when he first arrived in England.

James and Caroline, wedding day, 1939

Caroline with a slight smile at 5 foot 2 inches and 33 years of age and James[21] at 5 foot 4 inches and 42 years of age both appear smartly dressed and somber on their wedding day. Like many English Jews, James and Caroline took on many of the characteristics of the British[22] including being sober, dignified and punctual to family events. One area where many Polish Jews did not bend is marrying outside the faith. As we will see, this is one area where James and Caroline were quite narrow-minded.

James was living[23] with Caroline on the 2nd floor of her sister's Hannah Ferman's house on 32 Fontayne Road in Hackney London in 1945 (with his son Bernard), in 1946 (with son Bernard and daughter Eva) and in 1947 (with daughter Eva).

32 Fontayne Road Hackney London, where James and Caroline lived
1945-1947

Sylvia Sarah Rosen, James third and youngest daughter, was born approximately two years after James married Caroline in London, England (1941). Unfortunately, WW2 broke out and Caroline was evacuated to the countryside for safety while pregnant. When Sylvia was approximately six months old, Caroline went back to London to work and Sylvia lived with a woman and family for approximately five years. Sylvia recalled visits from James who would ride his bike out to the countryside from London to visit her. James and Caroline would also make visits during the summer. When the war ended, Sylvia was brought back to London to live with James, Caroline and her half-brother Reggie.

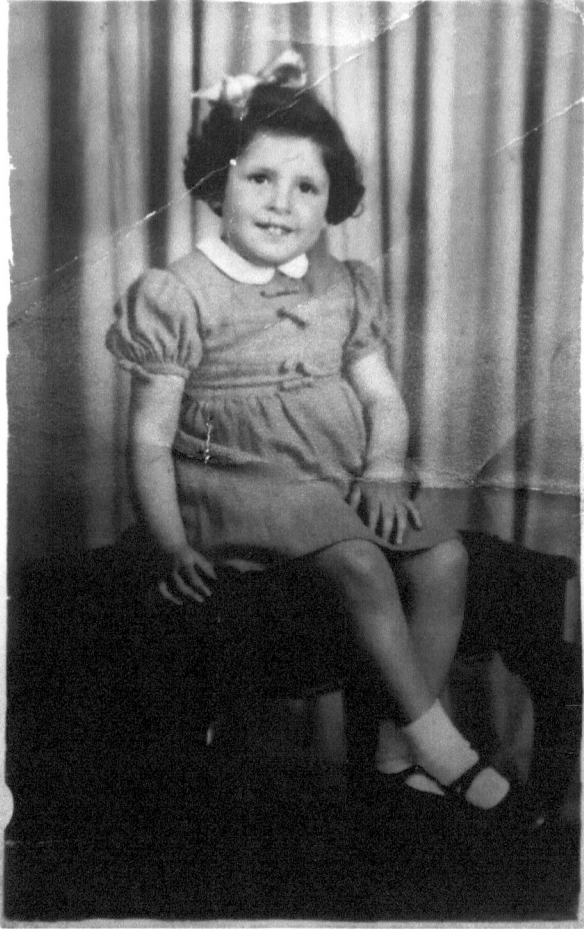

Sylvia circa 1940s

Sylvia remembered James as a very loving father when she was young. For example, he would carry plums with him when they would ride on the London trolley and give them to her when she would inevitably get motion sickness. Unfortunately, James changed towards Sylvia when she became a teenager and she became fearful of him. She describes James as a loving father, but a very strict, quite racist, and a stubborn man when she was young and a monster when she became an adolescent. Volatility erupted again when Sylvia married outside the Jewish faith. James and Caroline were angry that she married a Catholic and refused to attend the wedding.

Sylvia only communicated to James and Caroline through letters from 1957-1960 as she had moved to Virginia with her husband, John, who had joined the navy. When Sylvia returned, all was forgiven on both sides and she reported that James was a loving grandfather to 2-year-old Debra.

James early separation from his family, his immigration to a foreign country, his attempt to stay under the radar in an antisemitic climate, his experience living and serving in WW1 and WW2, the terrible loss of losing his first wife and his attempt to raise his children alone all likely contributed to his fierce stubbornness, deep racism, and unpredictable volatile personality.

---

1. Sources for family genealogy documents in this chapter can be found in Part II James, Sarah and Caroline family summary
2. London electoral records
3. Google map image taken March 30, 2019
4. In Gartner, 1975, Jewish Immigrant in England, 1870-1914.
5. Gartner ibid
6. Gartner ibid
7. Charles Booth. London poverty maps from Inquiry into Life and Labour in London (1886-1903)
8. Lipman, 1990
9. Singer sewing machines were reasonable priced, $5 down payment and $2 a week for 40 weeks. Source: Wikipedia
10. ibid Garner, 1976
11. Gartner, ibid
12. Jewish Chronicle
13. For more details on James children, see Part II, James, Sarah and Caroline family summary.
14. Bunny served as an army pilot during WW2 and was shot down by the Nazis but survived. He married twice and had one son named Philip.
15. London Gazette, 15 February 1949. More about this bankruptcy in Chapter 4.
16. Check out Charts, Rosenwald Heart Disease, common health issue among Rosen(wald).
17. Interview with daughter Debra 2018
18. The names have been redacted and will be released after 100 years from their birth.
19. According to Sylvia and Caroline, James asked Caroline's sister, Martha (one year younger) on a date and she said no. James then asked Caroline on a date. Martha never married.
20. See Introduction

21. Sylvia recollected that James called Caroline 'tittles" while Caroline called her husband Jimmy. This is an archaic biblical word meaning the tiny dot on the i or j as in "nothing is done til the i is dotted and the t is crossed."
22. Lipman, 1990
23. 1945, 1946, and 1947 electoral registrars No electoral rolls or registrars available during the period of WW2.

4

REACHES AMERICA AND CUBA

He has brought us to this place and has given us this land, a land flowing with milk and honey.

— DEUTERONOMY 26:9

When daughter, Eva, asked James to come live with her in the US in December of 1951, James and Caroline along with his two youngest children (Reggie and Sylvia) left England aboard the Queen Mary[1] and arrived in New York on December 15, 1951. According to Sylvia, all but her mother Caroline suffered from terrible motion sickness on the 10-day-voyage to the US[2].

Queen Mary circa 1950s

Caroline and James, circa 1950s

James in the US

In the photo above, Caroline, fashionable as always, is wearing a stylish pair of glasses and presents with a somber smiling. James demeanor is changed from all his previous photos sporting a much more relaxed smile. Was James feeling safe from the antisemitism he experienced in Poland and during the wars? For many Jews, the US was the "promised land," a safe harbor from the antisemitism experienced elsewhere.

James brought his Singer sewing machine with him from England. According to his daughter Sylvia, he worked in Lawrence, MA as a master tailor of women's clothing and likely found similar tailoring jobs in the Boston area once he moved into the city. His wife Caroline eventually got a job as a fuller or hemmer of clothing. During the 8 years that James lived

n the US, he and Caroline moved nine times[3]. It is not clear if this had to
do with money troubles, his personal volatility or a combination.

James bankruptcy revisited

Recall from Chapter 2 that James filed bankruptcy with his oldest son
Bernard in 1948. The bankruptcy notice ran four times (Feb 1949, April
1949 and then again as a dividends notice in 1961) in *The London Gazette*.
The first notice in February 1949 is an *Application to Discharge* the
bankruptcy. At that point, a hearing date was set for March 1st 1949 (See
below).

> **APPLICATIONS FOR DISCHARGE.**
> SPEVACK, Jacob (commonly known as James
> Rosen), described in the Receiving Order as
> James Rosen, 220, Arlington Road, London,
> N.W.1, lately of 32, Fountayne Road, London,
> N.16, and lately carrying on business as J.
> Rosen, at 64, Christian Street, London, E.1.
> LADIES' TAILOR. Court—HIGH COURT OF
> JUSTICE. No. of Matter—384 of 1948. Day
> Fixed for Hearing—March 1, 1949. 11 a.m.
> Place—Bankruptcy Buildings, Carey Street,
> London. W.C.2.

The London Gazette, February 15th, 1949 p. 849 Application for Discharge

The second notice to appear in *The London Gazette* was on April 1949 under
Orders on the Application for discharge of the bankruptcy. The discharge
was suspended for one year to March 1950, "as proof that the bankrupt had
been guilty of misconduct" (See below). No notice appeared for discharge
of the bankruptcy on March 1950 or thereafter and James left for America
on November 1951.

SPEVACK, Jacob (commonly known as James Rosen), described in the Receiving Order as James Rosen, 220, Arlington Road, London, N.W.1, lately of 32, Fountayne Road, London, N.16, and lately carrying on business as J. Rosen, at 64, Christian Street, London, E.1. LADIES TAILOR. Court—HIGH COURT OF JUSTICE. No. of Matter—384 of 1948. Date of Order—March 1, 1949. ·Nature of Order made—Bankrupt's discharge suspended for one year and that he be discharged as from March 1, 1950. Grounds named in Order for refusing an absolute Order of Discharge—Proofs of Facts mentioned in Section 26, sub-section 3, (A. and C.), Bankruptcy Act, 1914, as amended by Section 1 of the Bankruptcy (Amendment) Act, 1926, and whereas it has been proved that the bankrupt has been guilty of misconduct in relation to his property and affairs.

The London Gazette, April 8th, 1949, pgs. 1798-1799, Orders made on

Applications for discharge

The third notice related to this bankruptcy appeared in *The London Gazette* one year after James died in March 1961 as an *Intended Dividends* notice, notifying debtors that dividends were available for arrear payments (See below).

SPEVACK, Jacob (commonly known as James Rosen), described in the Receiving Order as James Rosen, of 220, Arlington Road, London, N.W.1, lately of 32, Fountayne Road, London, N.16, and lately carrying on business as J. Rosen, at 64, Christian Street, London, E.1, LADIES TAILOR. Court—HIGH COURT OF JUSTICE. No. of Matter—384 of 1948. Last Day for Receiving Proofs—28th March, 1961. Name of Trustee and Address—Walter, Arthur Aaron, Bankruptcy Buildings, Carey Street, London, W.C.2, Official Receiver.

The London Gazette, March 14th, 1961, p. 1964, Intended Dividends

The fourth and final notice appeared in *The London Gazette* one year after James died (1960) in May of 1961as a Final Dividend notice. This final notice is directed at vendors seeking arrear payments with less than one American dollar left in the Dividends account (See below).

SPEVACK, Jacob (commonly known as James Rosen), described in the Receiving Order as James Rosen of 220, Arlington Road, London, N.W.1, lately of 32, Fountayne Road, London, N.16, and lately carrying on business as J. Rosen, at 64, Christian Street, London E.1, LADIES TAILOR. Court— HIGH COURT OF JUSTICE. No. of Matter— 384 of 1948. Amount per £—5s. 10$\frac{7}{10}$d. First or Final, or otherwise—First and Final. When Payable—15th May, 1961. Where Payable—Bankruptcy Buildings, Carey Street, London, W.C.2.

The London Gazette, May 15th, 1961, p. 3400, Dividends

It is unclear if James ever paid his debtors by March 1950. That James was engaged in some misconduct related to the bankruptcy was not surprising to his daughter Sylvia nor to his granddaughter, the author, at this point. Was James required to pay the debts due to his misconduct? It remains unclear but it is quite coincidental that James traveled to America within one year of when these debts were due. Perhaps, James used that money to bring his family to America and then traveled to Cuba to see his siblings. We leave it to the reader to decide if this was a low-level scallywag move.

James travels to Cuba

In 1952, less than one year after arriving in the US and eight years before his death, James took a solo trip to Cuba to visit his siblings. He stayed with his oldest sister, Itta, during his visit to Cuba. Rosa's daughter, Fanny[4] recalls James visit and named her first son, James Imiak, after him. Sadly, James never told his daughter Sylvia who was 10 years old at the time or presumably his remaining children, about their family in Cuba. Below is a picture of James (bottom right) with his youngest sister, Rosa (bottom left) and his niece Fanny (top right).

L to R) Rosa, James, (front), Fanny and Fanny's husband (back)
during James' 1952 Cuba visit

Another photo of James in Cuba shows him wearing glasses with an open smile. Contrary to photos from England, and similar to US photos, James appears relaxed and happy.

James in Cuba, 1952

Our exploration of our grandfather James, aka Jacob Rosenwald, led to many surprises. We found our grandfather and his life was not anything like we expected to find. James was a scallywag, a deeply traumatized and flawed man, a good man, a loved husband, son, brother and father who died too early to know his grandchildren.

1. The Queen Mary was originally a WW2 transport ship converted to a luxury liner that sailed for more than 90 years. https://www.queenmary.com/history/ timeline/the-creative-years/

2. USA Declaration of Intention document for Caroline Rosen, Certificate Number A8 187 316
USA Declaration of Intention document for James Rosen, Certificate Number A8 187 437

3. Interviews by Debra with mother Sylvia in 2018 and 2019 and Naturalization records
List of places James and family lived when they arrived from England.

- 1952—40 Olive Ave., Lawrence, MA
- 1953—Uphams Corner, Dorchester, MA
- 1953-1955—3 Whittier St., Cambridge, MA
- 1955—Windsor St., Cambridge, MA
- 1956—Green St., Cambridge, MA
- 1956—14A Cherry St., Somerville, MA
- 1957—229 Franklin Street, Cambridge, MA
- 1960—Orchard Ave., Cambridge, MA
- 1960--Chester St., Central Square, Cambridge, MA

4. Phone-interview, Debra in 2018 while Fanny was in FL nursing home. Her son Salomon provided Spanish-English translation for hour-long conversation.

PART II

GENEALOGICAL FAMILY SUMMARIES

Sarah Rueben m. James Rosen m. Caroline Franks

- Bernard Rosen m. Eileen A.T. Harcus
  - living son
- Hetty Rosen m. William Maddock
  - Cecila Rosen (d. 3 years old)
  - Carol Maddock m. unknown
    - living son
    - living daughter
- Harry Lipton m. Eva Rosen m. Arnold Tertis
  - living daughter
  - living son
- William Rosen m. unknown
  - 5 children names unknown
- Stanley Rosen (Rueben)
- Reginald Rosen m. living
  - living daughter
    - living daughter
    - living son
    - living son
      - living son
      - living son
- Sylvia Rosen m. John Harkins Jr
  - Debra Harkins m. living
    - living son
      - living daughter
      - living daughter
  - Marsha Harkins m. living
    - living daughter
      - living daughter
      - living son
    - living son
      - living son
      - living son
      - living daughter

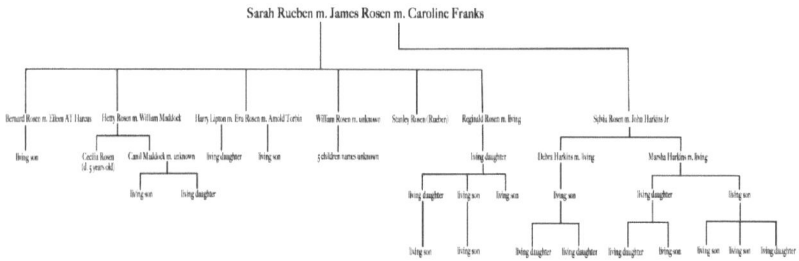

5

PARENTS SURA AND MENDEL

James Parents: Sura and Mendel Rozenwald
Family Summary [1]

SURA LIBA GUTESWILEN was born in Ciechanow, Poland/Russia in 1877 and died in 1945 of heart disease in Havana, Cuba at the age of 72. Sura was the daughter of Itta RUBINSTEJN and Pinches Guteswilen and had two siblings: Laja and Wolff. Sura's father, Pinches Guteswilen was the son of Liba Sura FILUT (parents Ruchia SILWKA and Dawid Filut) and Abram Guteswilen and had six siblings: Icek Levek (c. 1855); Hana Haja Sura; Szmul Jankief Jarlik (c. 1850); Ruchia Itta Jarlik; Manas Wisna (c. 1840); and Brucha Wisna. Pinches' father, Abram's parents were Brucha (c. 1769-1839; parents Lefek and Bryla) and Berket Guteswilen (c. 1773-1843; parents Ruchia and Szulim). Abram's was the brother of three siblings: Ruchia; Jankief; Icek Berkowicz (c. 1812-1852); and Mosiek Szulimowiz Guteswilen. Sura's sister, Laya had 3 sons: Abraham Gutesvilen in 1898 (no father mentioned, brother Barukla brought the baby boy to town office); Leisor Joiel Gutesvilen was born in 1900 (no father mentioned, Shlyama Zelek Shrum (55 years old) brought the baby boy to town office), Liesor died in 1911 at age 11; Zelek Gutesvilen born in 1902 (no father mentioned, Layla father, Pinches, brought the baby boy to town office). Sura's brother, Wolff (c. 1864-1910) married Blima Tyton and they had two children: Ruchia Itta Tyton (c. 1889) and Marian Sura Tyton (c. 1893).

James Mother
SURA LIBA GUTESWILEN
Direct Ancestors

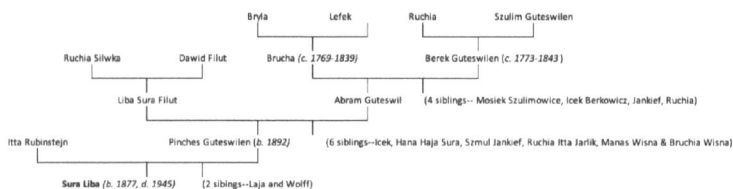

| Bryla | Lefek | Ruchia | Szulim Guteswilen |

On 18 June 1896, Sura married MENDEL ROZENWALD in Ciechanow, Poland. James father, Mendel, was born in Lukow, located in the Gubernia of Siedlce, Province of Lublin, Poland/Russia in 25 March 1867 and died of infection from a stab wound to the abdomen in 1944 in Havanah, Cuba at the age of 77. Mendel was the son of Sejzndla MALCMAN and Gerszon Rojzenwald. Like Mendel, his father Gerszon was born in Lukow, Siedlce, Poland/Russia in 1841. Gerszon's mother's name was Hinda (born in 1813) and his father's name was Israel (born in 1812). Mendel's mother Szejzndla married Herszko (Gerszon) in Lukow, Poland/Russia in 1865.

James Father
MENDEL ROZENWALD
Direct Ancestors

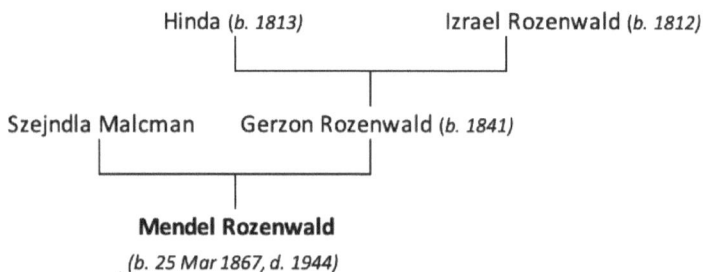

Hinda (b. 1813)   Izrael Rozenwald (b. 1812)

Szejndla Malcman   Gerzon Rozenwald (b. 1841)

Mendel Rozenwald
(b. 25 Mar 1867, d. 1944)

Mendel Rozenwald's birth record

Sura and Mendel marriage certificate, extraction and translations

(JRI-Poland)

Type	Year Recorded	ACT	Date of Marriage	Given name(s)	SURNAME	Age	Sex	Status / Profession	Father's Given Name	Mother's Given Name	Mother's Maiden SURNAME	Town Living In	Permanent Residence (Town)	Town born	Supplemental I
M	1896	23	18-Jun-1896	Mendel	ROZENWALD	20	m	single	Gerszon	Szajndla	MALCMAN	Siedlce			Banns - 11, 1 KERSZENBA
M	1896	23	18-Jun-1896	Sura Liba	GUTISWILEN	18	f	single	Pinches	Itta	RUBINSZTEJN	Ciechanów		Ciechanów	Banns - 11, 1 KERSZENBA

Sura and Mendel had five children[2], three boys (James, Adolf and Henry) and two daughters (Itta and Rosa). James was the oldest sibling followed by Adolf, Henry, Itta and Rosa was the youngest and most of Sura and Mendel's children were likely born in Warsaw, Poland. Unfortunately, almost all Jewish records of that period were destroyed during WW2 by Nazis, so we have no birth records for James and his siblings.

Sura Liba Guteswilen m. Mendel Rozenwald (m. 1896, Poland)

| James (b. 1897, d. 1960) | Adolf (b. 1900) | Henry aka Chaim (b. 1906, d. 1985) | Itta (b. 1919, d. 1983) | Rosa (b. 1911, d. 1986) |

Sura Liba Rosenwald grave in Havana, Cuba. Note, Borris Fisch died before he was 6 months old and was the son of Sura's oldest daughter, Itta.

1. Information extracted by ancestry.com translating expert in July 2018
2. Sibling information reported to Debra Harkins from Itta's daughter, Ruth Fisch Padorr, February 25, 2019

6

SIBLINGS ADOLFO, ITTA, HENRY AND ROSA

James siblings family summaries
Adolf, Itta, Henry, and Rosa

Adolf Rosenwald family summary

ADOLF ROZENWALD (aka Itche Lieb/Abram/Adolfo) was born circa August 3, 1900[1] in Poland/Russia.

Unfortunately, Adolf disappears from all records but likely served in WW1 and WW2. Unfortunately, over 60% of military service records were destroyed from enemy bombing in 1940 during WW2. Hence, there is no way to prove this conjecture except for Adolf's disappearance from all records and his sudden appearance on ship manifests in 1945, right as WW2 ended. A postcard photo of Adolfo with James Rosen, written in Yiddish, from Adolf to his mother assures her that her beloved son Avraham Yankel was alive and well. The photo[2] was likely taken in England between the wars and suggests that Adolfo was in contact with his family and James (Yankel) during this time. Adolf's travels beginning in 1945 suggests that he took up permanent residence in Cuba after the war, but the travel bug was strong in him.

Adolfo married Josefina Borges (45 years his junior) and had one son. The first record of Adolf is on a ship manifest list when he entered Miami, Florida on April 16, 1945 traveling from Havana, Cuba. On June 23, 1945, Adolfo traveled by ship from Cuba to Miami Florida with his final destination listed as New York City. He indicated that he planned to stay at the New Yorker Hotel. Adolfo is not found traveling again until August 23,1955 where he again traveled from Cuba to Florida and indicated on a manifest list that he is going to the Taft Hotel in New York City. Adolf likely lived in NYC for approximately 10 years between 1945-1955 where he owned a furniture store in Brooklyn, NY.[3]

In 1956, Adolfo is found on manifest lists making trips again from Cuba to New York via Miami, Florida with four other short 1-2-day trips from Cuba to Miami, Florida presumably these were business trips. Adolfo makes these same boat excursions three times in 1957. On one of these trips, Adolfo is traveling with his wife Josefina and their five-year-old son Manuel Mendel in June of 1957. Adolfo later is found on manifest lists traveling alone again making the same trip twice in 1958 and twice in 1959. Manifest lists reveal that Adolfo made at least 16 trips from Cuba to Florida between 1945 and 1962.[4]

With Cuba's revolution and Castro's overthrow of the government and the start of communism, Adolfo's travel to and from Cuba and Florida began to get more encumbered. In1960 he traveled once more with his wife from Cuba to Florida perhaps seeking a way out of the political turmoil brewing in Cuba. By 1962, Adolfo is tagged as a "parolee" by US Customs when he travels from Habana Cuba to Miami, Florida likely because he is now considered a citizen of a communist country. As a result, a US alien case file is created and records both his permanent address in Cuba as Ayuntamiento No. 155 Habana Cuba and his destination address in the US as 208 SW 1st Street, Miami, Florida.

Adolfo with his wife Sarah

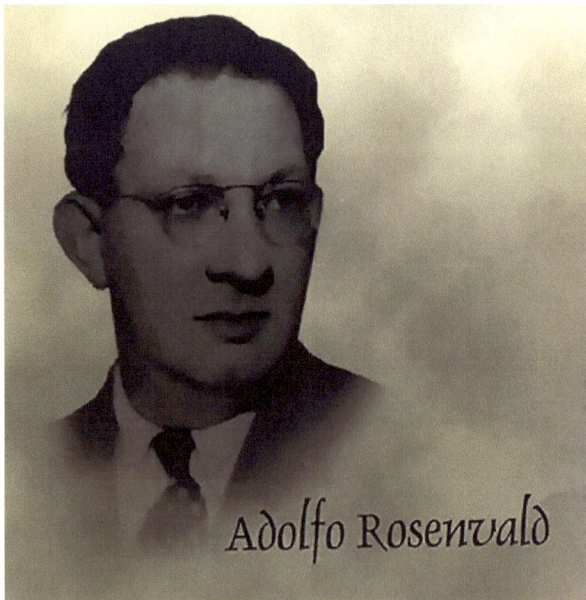

The last recorded trip Adolfo made was on August 3,1964 via Pan American Airlines from the USSR to Miami, Florida which suggests that in his 60s like many of us (and your author here), he was seeking to learn more about his genealogical roots. Evidence to support this hypothesis is a US Index to an Alien Case file that was created again due to his citizenship in then communist Cuba. Adolfo is listed as Adolfo Rosenwald Gotesvilen.[5] This is the only recorded document where Adolfo lists his mother's maiden as part of his name. Adolfo was finally naturalized[6] as a US citizen on Mar 18,1966 and died two short years later at the age of 69 in Brooklyn, NY.

Itta Rosenwald family summary

ITTA ROZENWALD (aka Christina, aka Ida) was born on April 7, 1910 in Warsaw, Poland. Itta married Abraham Uscher Fische 7 June 1926 in Havana, Cuba at the age of 16. Itta had seven children. She arrived in Florida on 3 June 1960 and died of heart disease on January 1, 1983 at the age of 73 in Miami, Florida. Itta is buried at Lakeside Memorial Cemetery in Miami, Florida.

The following is from Itta's daughter, Ruth Fisch Padorr, regarding Itta's 4 boys who died before the age of 6 months:

> *I found two pictures of graves in Cuba: Sura Liebe's and my brother Boris'. When I was there in 1997, I went to the cemetery. I have 3 other brothers buried there, but could not find them and actually, other than a picture of Boris' that I got when my parents died, do not have anything of the other three. Isaac was supposedly 3 months old and a set of twin boys (know nothing about them). The little I heard was that they all died of encephalitis, but it could be a disease that affects Jewish babies who do not last more than 6 months.*

Gravesite lists Borris Fisch death in 1934. Ruth continued:

> *My mother married when she was 15 and my dad was 18. Itta was 16 years old when she had Sol. She died of heart problems on Jan 1st 1983 at the age of 72 . She and dad are buried at Lakeside Cemetery located in NW 25th Street, Miami, FL. My dad, Abraham*

Uscher Fisch, died on April 13,1991. He died in Chicago after living with me for seven years after my mom died.

I.   SOLOMON FISCH was the oldest, born a year after my parents married and when my mother was 16. He became a doctor and practiced cardiology in NYC. He had four children. He suffered from Alzheimer's and remained in his home with his wife, until he died. He died at his home in Englewood Cliffs, NJ.

II.   RALPH FISCH was born on July 4, 1937 in Cuba. He married and had 3 children.

III.   RUTH FISCH PADORR *was born November 9, 1941 in Cuba and married Alan J Padorr on April 1, 1962 and they had two children. Alan was an electrical engineer and died on April 10, 1991. We lived in Chicago and Deerfield, IL and I remained in our home in Deerfield until 1997 when I moved to Florida to work for another company. I got my BA and MBA at night and weekends while working full time for Stepan Company. The company sponsored my education. I took early retirement in 2001 and bought my house in Palm Beach Gardens in PGA National near my brother Ralph. Stuart Creggy was introduced to me by my cantor. Stuart was born in London, England, was a lawyer and a magistrate there and had a winter home in Palm Beach. We married on May 18, 2008.*

Itta with husband Abraham Fische

(L to R) Itta's daughter Ruth, sons Ralph and Sol, Itta and husband Abraham
Fische

Henry Rozenwald family summary

HENRY ROZENWALD (aka Chaim/Gersz/Enrique) was born on 23
March 1906 in Warsaw Poland. Unfortunately, Henry is missing from all
birth, military and marriage records but family legend is that 16-year-old

Henry did not travel with his parents and younger siblings to Cuba in 1922. Instead, Henry may have been apprenticed to a relative in England or Canada. Henry may have served in WW2 like his older brothers but the destruction of military records in 1940 make this impossible to confirm. Similar to his brother Adolfo, Henry begins to appear in documents including the photo below with his niece Ruth Padorr and 2nd wife in 1958 in Cuba. In the first photo, Note, Henry is approximately 52 years old in this photo with a receding hair line and wearing formal attire.

Henry with 2nd wife Sarah and Itta's daughter Ruth Fische (15 yo)
in Havana, Cuba, circa 1958

According to his niece, Ruth Padorr[7], Henry first married "*Julia who died in Cuba of a breast cancer in 1955 and then married a Sephardic woman named Sarah.*" Sarah and Henry moved to Miami and opened a small store on 5th Street in Miami Beach, Florida selling clothing and accessories to elderly and immigrants. He died of heart attack November 1985[8] at the age of 79 in Miami Beach, Florida, United States. He is buried at the same cemetery as his sister Itta, Lakeside Memorial Cemetery in Miami, FL with his wife Sarah.

Rosa Rozenwald family summary

ROSA ROZENWALD[9] was probably born in 1911 in Warsaw, Poland. Around 1922, when Rosa was about 11 years old, Rosa's parents brought her to Cuba to escape the growing antisemitism raging in Poland. Rosa married twice, first to Salomon Novigrod and had three daughters: Esther, Ruth and Fanny. Rosa later divorced Salomon and married Isaac Godrodetsky. Rosa had a powerful presence in Havana especially with the business community.

Besides being a savvy business woman, Rosa was very moral as described by her niece, Ruth Padorr, and a loving mother and grandmother as described by her daughter, Fanny Novigrod. For example, on February 3, 1985, Rosa left Cuba and moved to Venezuela. This highly principled and family-oriented woman stayed in Cuba until her grandsons, Salomon and Abraham, were finally released from Cuba's forced labor camps. Most Jews had left Cuba, but Rosa stayed, probably to provide moral and emotional support for her family that still remained. One year later, knowing her family were safely out of Cuba, tired and worn, Rosa died of cardiac arrest at the age of 75. This loving woman is buried in Venezuela.

I. ESTHER NOVIGROD died at age 5 from an infection for which her father, Salomon, refused to take her to the hospital. Rosa never forgave her husband and divorced him shortly after.

II. RUTH NOVIGROD was born October 23, 1931 in Cuba and married Solomon Halfon and they had two daughters. Ruth and her husband owned a furniture store in Havana Cuba. In 1964, when the Cuban government took over the family's Havana store, Ruth, likely frustrated and angry, left Cuba and moved to the US. Ruth, like her mother Rosa, had a strong sense of family and moral principles and fought tirelessly for the release of her nephews, medical doctors Salomon and Abraham Imiak who were forced to work in the labor camps in Cuba. This feisty woman continued for over 16 years trying to get her nephews out of Cuba. Ruth eventually received help from the Houston Congressman Liman who spoke to Castro on the family's behalf. Thanks to Ruth and Congressman Liman, Salomon and Abraham were released from Cuba to the US in 1985 representing the first time that Castro allowed military Cubans to leave the country[10]. This amazing woman suffered for 15 years with Lymphoma cancer and died from a recurrence on May 28, 2009[11] and is buried in a Jewish cemetery in Houston, TX.

III. FANNY NOVIGROD born in Cuba, married and had three sons. Fanny left Cuba with her husband and oldest son for Argentina in 1983. She lived in Venezuela and currently lives in the US.

Rosa Rosenwald

James sister Rosa (r) and her daughter Fanny (l)

1. Although there are no birth records, this year is listed on the records of Adolfo's many plane and boat trips taken between Cuba and Florida in the years between 1945 and 1962.
2. Photo found among James 2nd wife personal belongings.
3. Source: Debra's interview (April 29, 2019) with Roberto Cohen (husband of Rosa's granddaughter Esther Halfron) who knew Adolfo and met with him several times in NYC.
4. The National Archives at Washington, D.C.; Washington, D.C.; Series Title: Passenger and Crew Lists of Vessels and Airplanes Arriving at Miami, Florida.; NAI Number: 2771998; Record Group Title: Records of the Immigration and Naturalization Service, 1787
5. US Index to Alien Case Files at National Archives in Kansas City, 1944-2003, Registration Number 12898989.
6. Adolf (Abraham) Rosenwald, Naturalization record, Miami, FL, Registration Number 1206826
7. As reported to Debra Harkins by Ruth Padoor via email in February and March of 2019
8. Source: Social Security (SSDI) death record.
9. All information here gathered by Debra through phone interview with Fanny Novigrod (Rosa's youngest daughter) Fanny's son Sal translated Spanish/English while Fanny was in nursing home in February 2019.
10. Abraham and Solomon reunite with family after 21 years https://apnews.com/ffcc59e11a11d56466995bf5fc8b7c0b
11. As reported to Debra Harkins via Rosa's daughter Fanny through
12. English/Spanish translation in March of 2019

7

WIVES SARAH AND CAROLINE AND CHILDREN

James, wives and descendants family summary

James, (aka Jacob, aka Avraham Yankel) was born on June 15 ,1897 probably in Siedlce, Poland and died on June 27, 1960 of a heart attack at the age of approximately 63 years[1]. He lived with his 2nd wife, Caroline at 79 Orchard St, Cambridge, MA at the time of his death and was buried at Ashkgnaz

Cemetery in Everett, MA on June 30, 1960. James was the son of Sura Liba (Guteswilen) Rosenwald and Mendel Rosenwald (both originally from Poland who later moved to Cuba) and was the older sibling of Adolfo, Henry, Itta, and Rosa.

James married his first wife SARAH REUBEN on Sept 1, 1918 in

St. Marylebone, London.[2] They had six children: Bernard, William, Helen, Eva, Stanley, and Reginald. Sarah Reuben was the daughter of Benjamin Reuben and Debra Benezon. She was born on July 6, 1893 in St James Westminster, London. Sarah died at age of 41 on April 16, 1937 of heart failure during an operation to fix a uterine prolapse.[3]

Children of Sarah and James

BERNARD B. ROSEN was born in Marylebone London on 30 May 1919[4] and died of heart failure in Jan of 1985 in Rhyll, Wales at the age of 65.[5] He lived at 20 Barrington Road, London and was buried in Wales. Barnard (Bunny) married in Stepney London in 1960[6] and had one son. Barnard lived at 12 Philson Mansion Raven Road, Stepney London from 1962-

1965.[7] Barnard lived with Brenda from 1963-1965 at 20 Winchester Place, Barrington Road, Crouch End, Hornsey County, London. Barnard married Brenda V in 1970 in Croyden, Greater London.[8]

According to family lore, Bernard was a pilot who fought in WW2 against the Nazis. He was shot down in Italy and lived with an Italian family where he learned to speak Italian. Bernard married twice (Eileen and Brenda) and had one son, Phillip, with his first wife Eileen. Bunny made at least one visit to the US with his 2nd wife Brenda and spent most of his time with his sisters Sylvia and Eve. Sylvia described her brother Bunny as a very generous man who fully paid all expenses for a 10 day visit to London. Bunny and his wife Brenda graciously had Sylvia stay with them and showed her around London for her entire stay. Bunny went into business with his father James, they had a falling out and bankruptcy ensued. It is believed they did not speak again.

HETTY H. ROSEN was born in Marylebone, London in 1921[9] and died 27 August 2000 in Ontario, Canada at the age of 79.[10] Hetty (Helen) had her first child, Cecilia Rosen (with James) in 1940 in Oxford, Oxfordshire.[11] Helen married William WJ Maddock in 1942 in Bedfordshire, England. Cecilia was born with Down's syndrome and died at 3 years of age in September 1943 in Wordsworth, London.[12] Helen and Bill had one daughter, Carol Lynne Maddock, who was born 1944 in Whitchurch, Shropshire, England.[13] Carol married and died at the age of 55 in Dartmouth, Nova Scotia. Carol had a son and daughter.

EVA ROSEN was born in West St. Pancras, London on June 30, 1924 and died of heart failure on November 11, 2001 in Anna Jacques Hospital in Newburyport, MA at the age 77. Eve was only 13 years old when she lost her mother. She enlisted in the military five years later on March 20th 1942 at the age of 18 and served until April 11, 1946. Eve served in the Royal army during World War 2, serving in the military in the London area B Corp. No 2 Central S/D. Eve enlisted 20 March 1942 and served until 11 April 1946.[14] Eve attained the rank of Corporal and was highly spoken of by her commanding officer as noted in her discharge booklet. Eve married Harry Lipton one year later in 1947 in Hackney England and moved to the

US in 1950 and had one daughter.[15] After the sudden death of Harry when her daughter was only one year old, Eve asked James to move to the US, which he did with 2nd wife Caroline, youngest son Reggie and youngest daughter Sylvia in 1951. Eve later married again and had one son in 1964. She lived in Newburyport, MA and is buried at Temple Emanuel in Andover, MA.

WILLIAM ROSEN (Billy) was born in St. Pancras London in 1927.[16] Death unknown. He married and Sylvia believes he had five children. Billy came to US in 1963 when he was about 36. Sylvia recalls that he may have been arrested in NY for passing bad checks and sent back to the UK.

STANLEY DOUGLAS EDWIN ROSEN was born in St. Pancras London in December 11, 1929[17] and died of heart failure on 25 Sept 1975 in Lawrence, MA. at the age of 46. He lived in Lawrence, MA and is buried at Temple Emanuel in Andover, MA. After the death of Stanley's mother Sarah, his father, James, sent 8-year-old Stanley to live with Sarah's brother Arthur Reubens and wife Mariam (Jacobs) at 88 Bellwoods Ave, Toronto, Canada in July 1937. Sylvia recalls Stanley saying he was abused by his aunt and uncle and is one of the reasons he chose to never marry or have children. Stanley changed his named to *Arthur Stanley Rubins* on September 26,1951 days before he arrived in Buffalo, NY. Stanley moved to live with his sister Eve at 40 Olive Ave, Lawrence, MA, in 1952 at the age of 23. Stanley worked with his sister Eve's second husband, Arnold Torbin, at *AH Notini Tobacco* in Spruce Street, Methuen, MA until his death. Stanley served from 3 March 1953 to 23 February 1955 as a Corporal in the US Army. Upon discharge from the Korean war, he moved back to his sister's home at 3 Whittier St., Cambridge Mass. Stanley never married.

Stanley (L), with his Aunt Miriam and Uncle Arthur Reubens
who raised him in Canada from age 8

REGINALD LESLIE ROSEN was born in St. Pancras London in July of 1935[18] and died from an overdose of pills in April of 1971 in Brookline, MA at the age of 36.[19] He lived in Brookline, MA and was buried at Askenaz Cemetery in Everett, MA. Reginald lost his mother, Sarah, when he was 2 years old. He was evacuated during WWII to the English countryside from ages of 8-13 years and suffered from allergies and asthma while he lived on the farm. After the war, Reginald (Reggie) was brought to the US with his father, James, stepmother, Caroline, and half-sister, Sylvia, on 22 Dec 1951. In Sept 1952, Reggie's father and sister Eve had a big fight that led to his father, stepmother, and half-sister moving to Uphams Corner, Dorchester, MA. However, Reggie, age 15, continued to live with his sister Eve on Olive Street in Lawrence. At age 18, Reginald joined the US selective service on 21 July 1953 while he lived at 3 Whittier Street, Cambridge, MA.[20] By 24, Reginald received his US naturalization papers on 29 June 1959.[21] Naturalization records indicate he was living at 14A Cherry Street, Somerville, MA and had brown eyes and brown hair, was 5 feet 9 and 1/2 inches tall and weighed 150 pounds. Reggie had a gambling problem which may have contributed to his attempted suicide sometime between 1963 and 1965 with sleeping pills, while he was living with his stepmother, Caroline. At age 31, Reginald married in 1967 and had one daughter.[22]

Reggie around 9-years-old and in the military (L to R)

James and Caroline Franks

Two years after the death of his first wife Sarah, James married Caroline Franks in London England in 1939.[23] On their marriage certificate, for the first time James lists himself as Jacob Rosen and his father as Mendel suggesting he finally felt safer than when he had first arrived in England. James and Caroline moved to the US.[24] [25]

Child of Caroline and James

Sylvia Sarah Rosen, James third and youngest daughter, was born approximately two years after James married Caroline in London, England (1941).[26] Unfortunately, WW2 broke out and Caroline was evacuated to the countryside for safety while pregnant. When Sylvia was approximately six months old, Caroline went back to London to work and Sylvia lived with a woman and family for approximately five years. Sylvia recalled visits from James who would ride his bike out to the countryside from London to visit her. James and Caroline would also make visits during the summer. When the war ended, Sylvia was brought back to London to live with her parents

James and Caroline and her half-brother Reggie. Sylvia married in 1957 and had two children.

---

1. Death certificate of James Rosen, City of Boston, Certificate Number 492
2. Marriage certificate of Sarah Reuben and James Rosen, Certificate Number 9735
3. Death certificate of Sarah Reuben Certificate Number 8220577-1
4. Bernard's birth civil record, located in Marylebone District, London, Vol 1a, pg. 638
5. Bernard's death record, Reg district Rhuddlan, Clwyd County, Vo 24, p. 813
6. Bernard's marriage record to Eileen Harcus, 1960, County of Stepney, Vol 5d, p. 1101
7. Bernard, electoral register, 1964, living with Brenda at 20 Winchester Place, Barrington Road, Ward Crouch End, County Hornsey
8. Bernard's 2nd marriage record with Brenda V, in 1970, District Croydon, County Greater London, Vol 5a, p. 1587
9. Hetty's birth record, District Marylebone, London, Vol 1a, p. 873.
10. Hetty's death record, 2000, North York, Ontario, Canada
11. Hetty's child, Cecilia birth record, 1940, District Oxford, County Oxfordshire, Vol 3a, p. 3513
12. Hetty's child Cecilia's death record, Sept 1943, District Wordsworth, County London, Vol 1d, p. 293
13. Hetty's child, Carol L. Maddock birth record, District Whitchurch, Shropshire County England 1944, Vol 6a, p. 1324
14. Eve military ID number, W126258
15. Eva's marriage record, Harry Lipton, 1947, District Hackney, London County, Vol 5c, p. 2011
16. William's birth civil record, Pancras District, London County, Vol 1b, p. 23
17. Stanley's US index to Alien Arrivals at a Canadian Atlantic Seaport record,, St. Albans, Vermont, 157
18. Reginald's birth record, 1935, District Pancras, London County, Vol 1b, p. 101
19. Reginald's death record, 1971, Brookline, MA, Vol 033, P. 502, Index Vol No. 158/159 , Reference Number F63.M363 v. 158/159, Reginald's Social Security claims index record, Claim date 4 May 1971
20. Reginald's US selective service record, certificate number 191735307
21. Reginald's US naturalization, US District Court, Certificate number 8107182, Reference number 341078, Reginald's record of SSN 022-26-9198 received MA (1951-1952)
22. Reginald's marriage certificate, Brookline MA, certificate number 442
23. Marriage certificate of Caroline Franks and James Rosen, Certificate Number MXH 255950
24. USA Declaration of Intention document for Caroline Rosen, Certificate Number A8 187 316
25. USA Declaration of Intention document for James Rosen, Certificate Number A8 187 437 of London, Certificate Number 8130213-1
26. Sylvia's birth record,1941, Hitchens Hertfordshire, Vol 3a, p. 1667

BIOGRAPHY

Gartner, L.L. 1969. *The Jewish immigrant in England, 1870-1914*. London: Ruskin House.

Kopowka, E. 2014. *The Jews in Siedlce: 1850-1945*. NY: JewishGen, Inc.

Levine, R. M. 2010. *Tropical Diaspora: The Jewish experience in Cuba*. NJ: Markus Wiener Publishers.

Liepman, V.D. 1990. *A History of the Jews in Britain since 1858*. London: Leicester University Press.

Polonsky, A. 2013. *The Jews in Poland and Russia: A Short history*. Littman Library of Jewish Civilization.

Stampfer, S. 1992. Gender differentiation and education of Jewish woman in 19th Century Eastern Europe. *Polin: Studies in Polish Jewry, 7*: 63-87.

Yassini, A. Wolff (Ed.) 2013. *Memorial (Yizkor) book for the Jewish Community of Ciechanow*. NY: JewishGen, Inc.

APPENDIX

Chapter 1

Newspaper report of Siedlce 1906 pogrom

Sierra of Aucland paper *https://sites.google.com/site/myjewishsiedlce/year-1906/mail-steamer-ant-aucland*

Advices received at St. Petersburg from Siedlce, Poland, are to the effect that fighting and the bombarding of houses, which ceased about midday on Monday, was resumed late in the afternoon, apparently in consequence of Governor Eugelke's demand that the Jewish and Polish populace deliver up to him members of the Jewish Self-defence Association. They refused, and, preferring death in the open to tame surrender, resumed the battle. Artillery was again brought into action. A Jewish massacre, surpassing in seriousness all previous ones in the vicinity, took place at Siedlce on Saturday and Sunday, 4th and 5th August. It was carefully planned beforehand, soldiers warning all of the Christian population in advance to hang out their ikons, so that they might remain undisturbed. On Saturday night some terrorists killed two soldiers, and thereupon the Libau Regiment broke forth in unrestrained fury. They began murdering Jews on every hand, and continued their work of slaughter all night Saturday and all day Sunday. The ghastly work of murdering and pillaging continued until early on the morning of the 10th, until Governor-General Skalton telegraphed for permission to use artillery. Four batteries then opened fire down Pienkna, Warsaw, and Aliena streets, which were inhabited by thousands of Jews. The destruction was horrible. As a result of the general slaughter, it is estimated that fully 200 Jews have been killed and 1000 wounded. There are 3000 prisoners in custody, a great many of whom are wounded. Not a soldier was killed. Squads of soldiers were afterwards parading through the streets selling pillaged watches and jewellery. Army officers openly-countenanced the selling of loot. The local Governor took no steps to prevent the outrage. To prevent reports of the outrages being sent, the telegraph offices were closed, and no persons were allowed to leave the town. Refugees crowded the stations. The soldiers were drunk and behaving with extraordinary brutality. A delegation of citizens asked the Governor to order the troops to cease firing, but the Governor replied that the citizens must

deliver up their leaders and or otherwise the city would The authorities asserted tha had arrived from Warsaw, would have to be arrested bef inhabitants were permitted t The scenes on the 9th and unspeakable horror. Eve were screams and cries, mi sound of shooting. Soldier restaurants of the Victoria F the furniture of the establish ried off wines and liquors. in the big bazaar of the cit adding terror to the killing which had been going on for quent shots and occasional vc heard in different parts of because of the general panic to learn accurately just what v There seems no doubt that are responsible for provokin by their fusillades from the dows on Saturday against tl policemen who were patrolli The troops surrounded the which this firing came, and leys through the windows ar was followed by a search o which soon developed into dering, and subsequently ii and slaughter. All the Jew been looted. The owners their property were killed Any person seen leaving a ing out of a window was mercy. Most of the prisone Jews, and they were beaten The Jews at Warsaw were attack.

Chapter 2

Name.	Corps.	Rank	Regtl. No.
ROSEN	R a S C	Dvr.	T/35233
Jim			

Medal.	Roll.	Page.		Remarks.
VICTORY	Rasc/101 B/49	15/60	B.	
BRITISH	do			
15 STAR	Rasc/6/B18.	5-63 9		

Theatre of War first served in	3.
Date of entry therein	2 4 3 . 15

K. 1390.

Correspondence.

Address.

(26454—14a) Wt. W 3347—H.P 6451 200m. 10/19 H. St Est. 5450/1256

(To be rendered in duplicate.)

ROYAL ARMY SERVICE CORPS. REGIMENT

M.W. ROLL OF INDIVIDUALS entitled to the Victory Medal and/or British War Medal granted under Army Orders

Regtl. No.	Rank	NAME	In sequence Units and Corps previously served with...	Theatres of war in which served	Claps awarded
T/35233	Dvr.	ROSEN Jin.	R.A.S.C. T/35233 Driver.		
T/35235	"	HASKELL John William.	R.A.S.C. T/35235 Driver.		
T/35239	a/Sgt	CAINES Harold Spencer.	R.A.S.C. T/35239 Driver.		
T/35240	Dvr	MARSH Alfred.	R.A.S.C. T/35240 Driver.		
T/35242	"	TAYLOR Bertie Alexander.	R.A.S.C. T/35242 Driver.		
T/35243	T/Sgt	HARDING Albert.	R.A.S.C. T/35243 T/Sergeant.		
T/35245	Dvr	COATES Fred.	R.A.S.C. T/35245 Driver.		
T/35259	"	WILLETT George Henry.	R.A.S.C. T/35259 Driver.		
T/35260	"	UTTLEY Joseph	R.A.S.C. T/35260 Driver.		
T/35262	"	MAJOR Victor Percival.	R.A.S.C. T/35262 Driver.		

I certify that according to the Official Records the individuals named in this ROLL are entitled to the

Place R.A.S.C. RECORD OFFICE WOOLWICH DOCKYARD
Date 25 SEP 1920
MEDAL SECTION.

(# 20 22) W1904—NP4022 80,000 7/10 HWV(R181) N2728
265—31P2178 50,000 4/20

(To be rendered in duplicate.)

ROYAL ARMY SERVICE CORPS.

Regiment or Co

ROLL OF INDIVIDUALS entitled to the Decoration granted unde

To be left blank	On date of Disembarkation		NAME		Date of Disembarkation	(a) (b) (c)
	Regtl. No.	Rank				
	T/35222	Dvr	KENDALL	W.	13-3-15 (3)	Di
	T/35223	"	MORGAN	F.	14-3-15 (2b)	D
	T/35225	"	HARRIS	R.	17-5-15 (3)	A
	T/35227	"	ROBERTS	S.	18-9-15 (1)	
	S/35229	Pte	TAYLOR	J.G.	16-12-14(1)	
	S/35230	"	BILLINGTON	J.	16-12-14(1)	
	T/35231	Dvr	BULL	T.	17-5-15 (3)	
	T/35233	"	ROSEN	J.	24-3-15 (3)	
	T/35236	"	AYLEY	E.W.	27-4-15 (2b)	
	T/35240	"	MARSH	A.	13-3-15 (3)Dis	
	T/35242	"	TAYLOR	B.A.	14-3-15 (2b)	A
	T/35243	"	HARDING	A.	10-7-15 (3)	

I certify that according to the Official Records the individuals named in this RO

Place ___ WOOLWICH DOCKYARD

Date ___ 6 - DEC. 1920 MEDAL SECTION

Chapter 3

James and Caroline religious and civil marriage documents

ABSTRACT OF THE כְּתֻבָּה

On the *first* day of the week, the

day of the month *Tebeth* , in the y

corresponding to the *24th* of *Dee*

the holy Covenant of Marriage was entered

between the Bridegroom— *Jacob oth*

and his Bride— *Caroline F*

The said Bridegroom made the following

Bride :

"Be thou my wife according to the law

Israel. I faithfully promise that I will be a

thee. I will honour and cherish thee; I will

will protect and support thee, and will p

necessary for thy due sustenance, even as it

husband to do. I also take upon mysel

obligations for thy maintenance, during thy

prescribed by our religious statute "

Chapter 4

United Ashenaz Cemetery[1], Everett, MA where James, Caroline and Reginald
Rosen are buried.

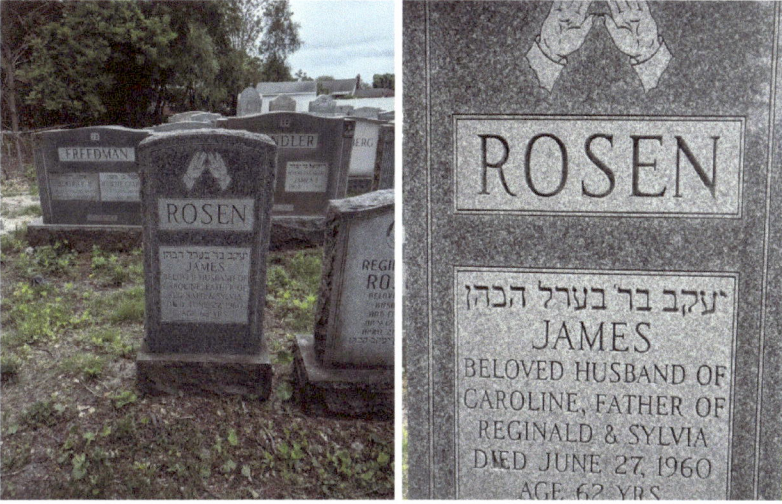

James Rosen (Jacob Rosenwald) buried at United Ashenaz Cemetery, Everett, MA

Reginald Rosen buried at United Ashenaz Cemetery, Everett, MA

Eve (Eva Rosen) Lipton Torbin buried at Temple Emanuel in Andover, MA

Arthur Stanley Rubins (Stanley Rosen) buried at Temple Emanuel in Andover, MA

---

1.   Gravestones are 3-4 rows back to left of entrance column.

www.ingramcontent.com/pod-product-compliance
Lightning Source LLC
Chambersburg PA
CBHW040936030426

42335CB00001B/10